# Mideast Treaty

## Greatest Prophetic
## Fulfillment in 2000 years

# Mideast Treaty

### Greatest Prophetic
### Fulfillment in 2000 years

# Irvin Baxter, Jr.

**endtime** is a Christian ministry that is dedicated to the service of the Lord Jesus Christ. Our purpose is to spread the word of His Gospel, to declare the truths of His existence, and to create an awareness of His soon return.

*A Message for the President* is published by **endtime** Incorporated. All rights reserved. Written permission must be secured from the publisher to use or reproduce any part of this book, except for brief quotations in applicable reviews or articles.

To obtain permissions write; **endtime**, PO Box 2066, Richmond, IN 47375-2066

Copyright © 1994 by **endtime** Incorporated

Library of Congress Catalog Number 94-70128
ISBN 0-941559-01-7

Printed in the United States of America

*To my wonderful church who was so understanding when I wasn't always available,*

*To the ENDTIME staff members who were so patient when deadlines were missed,*

*To my wonderful wife whose support has never waivered,*

*And to the Lord Jesus Christ to whose kingdom I pray this book will bring glory!*

# Preface

Every 2,000 years there is a major event in the plan of God for the human race. In 4000 B.C. Adam and Eve were created. In 2000 B.C. Abraham was born. He became the father of the physical people of God on earth—the Jews, and the spiritual people of God on earth—the Church. He also, through Ishmael, became the father of the Arabs (Moslems). Two thousand years later Jesus Christ was born.

We now find ourselves a few short years away from the next 2,000-year milestone. The rapid fulfillment of Bible prophecies that we are presently witnessing indicates that this juncture will be the most dramatic and pivotal turning point yet in God's plan for the earth!

The most important of these prophecies for our time is that a covenant concerning the status of Jerusalem will be signed and then confirmed. The confirming of this covenant begins a final seven-year period ending with the fateful Battle of Armageddon. Is it coincidence that on May 19, 1993, **exactly seven years before the year 2000**, the *Jerusalem Covenant* was signed?

# Contents

One of the prominent features of the government of the Antichrist will be a worldwide identification system and a cashless society. By these two things, every person will be brought under world government control.

The Bible states that there will be those on earth during endtime events that will understand exactly what is happening. This knowledge will result in great religious revival right in the middle of all the wickedness.

When the United Nation's armies come against Israel to bring her under subjection to the will of the world community, the Battle of Armageddon will be the result.

Jews believe that those buried on the Mount of Olives will be the first to raise from the dead when Messiah comes. It is at the time of Armageddon that both Jews and Christians will crown Jesus—King of kings and Lord of lords.

# 1

# Seven Years to Armageddon?

## Is the Israeli-PLO Agreement the beginning of the final seven years?

The Bible specifically prophesies a period of seven years which immediately precedes the world's last war, Armageddon. It is at Armageddon that Jesus Christ returns to earth to usher in His 1,000-year reign of peace.

During this seven year period, there will be more prophetic fulfillment than in any other comparable time period in the history of the world. The Jewish Temple will be rebuilt in Jerusalem, and animal sacrifices, as were conducted in the Old Testament, will be resumed. A world government will take control on earth, and a powerful politician will become a world dictator. Halfway through the seven years, the worst religious and political persecution of all time will begin. Jesus called this time the Great Tribulation.

This prophesied seven-year period will be started by the "confirmation" of a covenant. The two all-important questions we want to consider are: **1.** Is the *Jerusalem Covenant* signed on May 19, 1993, **the covenant** referred to in the prophecy? **2.** Was the signing of the Israeli-Palestinian agreement by Yasser Arafat and Yitzhak Rabin on September 13, 1993, the prophesied **"confirming"** of the covenant?!

The prophecy concerning the climactic seven years is found in Daniel 9:27:

> *"And he shall **confirm** the*
> ***covenant** with many for **one week**:*
> *and in the midst of the week **he***
> *shall cause the sacrifice and the*
> *oblation to cease, and for the over-*
> *spreading of **abominations** he shall*
> *make it **desolate**, even until the con-*
> *summation, and that determined*
> *shall be poured upon the desolate."*

There are five questions that must be answered if we are to understand this prophecy of Daniel 9:27: **1.** What is the Abomination of Desolation? **2.** How long is one week? **3.** Who is "he" that confirms the covenant? **4.** To what covenant does this refer? **5.** What is the "confirming" of the covenant?

If we can answer these five questions, we have discovered five keys that will unveil to us the most important prophetic fulfillment since the crucifixion of Jesus Christ.

# 2

# The Abomination of Desolation

"And he shall cause the sacrifice and the oblation to cease, and for the over-spreading of abominations he shall make it desolate."

Daniel 9:27

It is absolutely impossible for anyone to have a comprehensive understanding of endtime prophecy without thoroughly understanding what the Abomination of Desolation is. This event is referred to in both the Old and the New Testaments.

Jesus Christ spoke about the Abomination of Desolation in His famous Olivet Discourse in Matthew, chapter 24. His disciples were showing him Israel's beautiful Second Temple that had been built by Zerubbabel and enlarged and refurbished by Herod the Great. The Temple was the pride of the Jewish nation and the center of its religious life.

4

Jesus shocked the disciples by saying, "There shall not be left here one stone upon another, that shall not be thrown down" (Matthew 24:2). This provoked the disciples to ask these questions in verse 3: "Tell us, when shall these things be? and what shall be the sign of thy coming, and of the end of the world?" Jesus spent the rest of the 24th chapter of Matthew answering these three questions.

In verse 15 he commented on the event called the Abomination of Desolation: "When ye therefore shall see the abomination of desolation, spoken of by Daniel the prophet, stand in the holy place, (whoso readeth, let him understand:)".

When Jesus spoke of the Abomination of Desolation, he referred back to Daniel. However, Jesus included an additional piece of information not given in Daniel. He said the Abomination of Desolation would **stand in the holy place**. We'll learn more about that a little later.

Jesus went on to say in Matthew 24: "When you therefore see the abomination of desolation...then let them which be in Judea flee into the mountains: Let him which is on the housetop not come down to take any thing out of his house: Neither let him which is in the field return back to take his clothes. And woe unto them that are with child, and to them that give suck in those days! But pray ye that your flight be not in the winter, neither on the sabbath day: For **then shall be great tribulation** such as was not since the beginning of the world to this time, no, nor ever shall be."

This is a very critical point! When you see the Abomination of Desolation, **then** you need to flee.

5

If you live in the area of Jerusalem and Judea, flee into the mountains. If you are on your housetop, don't even come back down into your house to get your clothes; but immediately flee!

In verse 21 Jesus tells us why: "For **then** shall be **great tribulation** such as was not since the beginning of the world to this time, no, nor ever shall be." The prophesied Great Tribulation is a three and one-half year period of the greatest political and religious persecution in the history of the world. This three and one-half years of Great Tribulation will continue until the final Battle of Armageddon. Jesus said that the event called the Abomination of Desolation is the event that will trigger the Great Tribulation. This is vital for us to understand! Jesus didn't tell them to flee before the Abomination of Desolation. He told them to flee **when** they saw the Abomination of Desolation.

We've learned something very critical to our understanding of the chronology of endtime events. Remember that Daniel said in the midst (or middle) of the week, "he" shall place the abomination that maketh desolate. This is the same "Abomination of Desolation" to which Jesus Christ referred. Jesus told us that in the middle of the week the Great Tribulation will begin. Many have thought that the Great Tribulation begins at the beginning of the seventieth week of Daniel. Jesus himself specifically states here that the tribulation begins **in the middle** of the week. What this means to us is, there is no such thing as a mid-tribulation rapture. Either the rapture occurs before the Tribulation or after the Tribulation. If it occurs before the Tribulation, it can occur anytime up until the Abomination of Desolation. If it occurs after the Tribulation, it will occur around the time of the Battle of Armageddon.

The Apostle Paul reveals more details in his writings concerning this pivotal event called the Abomination of Desolation. His comments are found in II Thessalonians 2:1-4:

> *"Now we beseech you, brethren, by the coming of our Lord Jesus Christ, and by our gathering together unto him, that ye be not soon shaken in mind, or be troubled, neither by spirit, nor by word, nor by letter as from us, as that the day of Christ is at hand. Let no man deceive you by any means: for that day shall not come, except there come a falling away first, and that man of sin be revealed, the son of perdition; who opposeth and exalteth himself above all that is called God, or that is wor-shipped; so that he as God **sitteth in the temple of God**, shewing himself that he is God."*

The Apostle Paul refers to events that will occur around the time of the coming of the Lord Jesus Christ. He said, "That day shall not come except there come a falling away first." Many people think we must enter a period of backsliding from the church in these last times. However, this is not true. The falling away referred to here by the

7

Apostle Paul has already occurred. The early church started out in a blaze of glory and apostolic power. As apostasy set into the church, it began to decline. One doctrine after another was changed until the church descended into what has historically been called the Dark Ages. From approximately 500 A.D. until 1500 A.D. the average person didn't even have a Bible. Since the people could not read the word of God for themselves, and since the clergy had become corrupt, much error filled the churches. Paul referred to this time of the Dark Ages as the falling away.

When God spoke to Martin Luther that "the just shall live by faith", the climb out of the Dark Ages and back to the original state of the church began. From then until now, one truth after another has been restored to the church. Even as the early apostolic church was brought in with a blaze of glory, the last day church will go out at the time of the rapture with a mighty blaze of glory! We should not be looking for a great falling away now. We should be looking for the prophesied endtime revival! As Jesus Christ went up with a shout, he is coming back with a shout!

Paul states that there would be a falling away, and the man of sin, the son of perdition, would be revealed. The Man of Sin, the Son of Perdition, the Beast, and the Antichrist are all synonymous terms. These refer to the prophesied world dictator which shall rule the entire world right before the establishment of the Kingdom of God by Jesus Christ.

Verse 4 tells us what the Antichrist will do. It says he "Opposeth and exalteth himself above all that is called God, or that is worshipped; so that he as God sitteth in the temple of God, showing himself that he is God." When Jesus talked about the Abomination of Desolation in Matthew 24:15, he said the Abomination of Desolation would stand **in the holy place**. In II Thessalonians 2:4, the Apostle Paul talks about a time when the Antichrist will move **into the temple of God** and claim to be God. Paul and Jesus are both referring to the same event, the Abomination of Desolation.

At this present time there is no temple in Israel. However, there are many prophecies which teach that the Jewish Temple will be rebuilt in these last times. Daniel 9:27 states that, at the Abomination of Desolation, the Antichrist will make the sacrifice and the oblation to cease. He can't make it to cease unless it has first been reinstituted. We will show extensively later in this book that preparation is being made right now to resume animal sacrifices and temple worship in Israel.

The Abomination of Desolation is when the Antichrist breaks the covenant which he had confirmed three and one-half years before. He will make the Jewish animal sacrifice to cease and will sit in the rebuilt Jewish Temple proclaiming himself to be God. This blasphemous event will begin the Great Tribulation.

# 3

# The Future War in Heaven

"And there was war in heaven:
Michael and his angels fought against
the dragon; and the dragon fought and
his angels."

Revelation 12:7

## How long is "one week"?

We have previously shown that the Great
Tribulation period spoken of by Jesus occupies the
last half of Daniel's seventieth week. We need to
know how long one week is as used in this
prophecy.

Daniel 7:25 states:

> "And he shall speak great words
> against the most High, and shall
> wear out the saints of the most High,
> and think to change times and laws:
> and they shall be given into his
> hand until **a time** and **times** and the
> **dividing of time**."

This scripture gives a description of the Great Tribulation under the rule of the Antichrist. It specifically states here that the Antichrist will "wear out the saints" for a time and times and the dividing of time. A time is one year, times is two years, and the dividing of time is one-half year.

We know this because Revelation 13:5-7 teaches the Antichrist will make war with the saints for 42 months which equals three and one-half years:

> *"And there was given unto him a mouth speaking great things and blasphemies; and power was given unto him to continue **forty and two months**. And he opened his mouth in blasphemy against God, to blaspheme his name, and his tabernacle, and them that dwell in heaven. And it was given unto him to make war with the saints, and to overcome them: and power was given him over all kindreds, and tongues, and nations."*

Revelation 12:6 confirms in another way that the Tribulation will last for three and one-half years:

> *And the woman fled into the wilderness, where she hath a place prepared of God, that they should feed her there a **thousand two hundred and threescore days**.*

Three different descriptions of the length of the Great Tribulation are used: time, times, and the dividing of time; forty and two months; and one thousand two-hundred and sixty days. These all describe the same length of time—three and one-half years.

If the tribulation is three and one-half years long and occupies the last half of Daniel's seventieth week, then the first half of the week would also be three and one-half years. We can conclude then that, when Daniel spoke of one week, he was speaking of a week of years—a seven year period.

Many people have believed that the Great Tribulation is seven years long. This is not true as we have shown above. It is true, however, that the seventieth week of Daniel is seven years in length. The first half of this seven years is not tribulation at all. During this first three and one-half years, the Antichrist is ascending to power through peace and diplomacy. The last three and one-half years is the Great Tribulation which begins with the Abomination of Desolation and culminates with the prophesied final Battle of Armageddon.

## The War in Heaven

At the same time the Abomination of Desolation occurs, the Bible teaches there will be an angelic war in heaven.

In Revelation, chapter 12, the Bible describes a woman clothed with the sun. The woman was travailing in birth to bring forth a child. A great red dragon stood before the woman, who was ready to be delivered, with the intent of devouring her child as soon as it was born. The woman gave birth to a man child who was to rule the nations with a rod of iron, and her child was caught up unto God, and to his throne.

The woman is Israel, the child is Jesus Christ, and the dragon is Satan. When Jesus was born, Satan, in fact, did attempt to kill him. The wise men, traveling from afar to worship Jesus, stopped at Herod's palace attempting to find the King of the Jews that had been born. Herod knew nothing of Jesus but asked the wise men, when they found this King of the Jews, to return to him. Herod said that he too, would like to worship the newborn king. The Scriptures tell us that Herod actually did not want to worship Jesus, but to kill him.

The wise men did find Jesus, and fell down worshipping him. After presenting to the Christ their gifts of gold, frankincense, and myrrh, they departed into their own country. God had warned the wise men in a dream not to return to Herod.

When Herod saw that he was mocked by the wise men, he issued an order to kill all male children from the age of two years and down in the Bethlehem area. Before this, however, the angel of the Lord had warned Joseph in a dream to flee with the child to Egypt. Consequently, Satan's goal of killing the Savior of the world was thwarted. God is always one step ahead of the Devil and always will be!

Joseph and Mary lived in Egypt with their child Jesus for approximately two years. After this time, God again appeared unto Joseph, saying, "Arise, and take the young child and his mother, and go into the land of Israel: for they are dead which sought the young child's life." Joseph, Mary, and Jesus returned to Nazareth where Jesus spent the remainder of his childhood.

From this account we see how Satan did attempt to devour Jesus as soon as he was born; but God protected this child which is destined to rule all nations with a rod of iron.

In Revelation 12:7-10 we read about the war in heaven that will take place at the same time that the Abomination of Desolation occurs:

> "And there was war in heaven: Michael and his angels fought against the dragon; and the dragon fought and his angels, And prevailed not; neither was their place found any more in heaven. And the great dragon was cast out, that old serpent, called the Devil, and Satan, which deceiveth the whole world: he was cast out into the earth, and his angels were cast out with him. And I heard a loud voice saying in heaven, Now is come salvation, and strength, and the kingdom of our God, and the power of his Christ: for **the accuser of our brethren** is cast down, which **accused them** before our God day and night."

This war in heaven has not yet occurred. We know this because, as a result of this war, the accuser of the brethren will be cast down. The accuser of the brethren is not cast down right now.

In Job 1:6-12, when the angels came to present themselves before the Lord, Satan came also among them. The Lord said to Satan: "Hast thou considered my servant Job?" Satan made the accusation that Job only served God because of all the blessings that God had bestowed upon him. Satan was the accuser of Job in that day. He still is accusing God's people today. He wants to place us under the load of guilt and condemnation when there is "now no condemnation to them who are in Christ Jesus" (Romans 8:1).

When this war in heaven does take place, Satan is no longer going to have access to heaven, as he did in the days of Job, and as he does at this present time. The Bible says, "the accuser of our brethren is cast down, which **accused them before our God day and night**." Some have taught that this war in heaven took place before the creation of man. This cannot possibly be true because the above scripture explicitly states that before he was cast down, Satan accused the brethren before God day and night. Satan could not accuse brethren that didn't even yet exist. Furthermore, verse eleven states that "they overcame him by the blood of the Lamb, and by the word of their testimony." While Satan was accusing them, they overcame him by the blood of the Lamb, and they loved not their lives unto the death. This proves that this prophesied war will take place after Calvary because the blood of the Lamb is available to those who are being accused by Satan.

# What triggers this war?

Revelation 12:12 says concerning Satan: "The devil is come down unto you, having great wrath, because **he knoweth that he hath but a short time.**"

Satan has known from the beginning the amount of time he has to deceive the world. He knows that, from the fall of man to the ushering in of the Kingdom of God, there is to be approximately 6,000 years. That's why the demon cried out at Jesus in confusion, "Art thou come hither to torment us before the time?" (Matthew 8:29). Satan did not then understand that there were going to be two comings of Christ. He had no knowledge of the plan for divine redemption. He knew Jesus had come to earth 2,000 years early, but he didn't know why!

Satan does understand now. He knows today that we are only a few short years from the time when he will be bound in the bottomless pit for 1,000 years (Revelation 20:1-3). It is this knowledge that will drive him to make his futile attack on the armies of heaven.

Three and one-half years before Satan is cast into the bottomless pit, he will try once again to overthrow God from his throne in heaven and to take that rulership for himself. However, the archangel Michael and his army will fight against Satan, and Satan will be defeated. It is at this time that Satan is cast out of heaven and confined to the earth.

Revelation 12:12 says:

*"Therefore rejoice, ye heavens, and ye that dwell in them. Woe to the inhabiters of the earth and of the sea! For the devil is come down unto you, **having great wrath**, because **he knoweth that he hath but a short time.**"*

When Satan realizes that he once again has been defeated, he will be exceedingly angry. He will know at this point that he only has three and one-half years left in which to work. In the evil of his imagination, he will still believe that he can defeat the Almighty God. He will launch his plan to accomplish on earth what he has been unable to achieve in heaven. He will launch the Great Tribulation. The Great Tribulation will be the wrath of Satan. The wrath of God will be immediately after the Great Tribulation. Matthew 24:29 teaches us this:

*"**Immediately after the tribulation** of those days shall the sun be darkened, and the moon shall not give her light, and the stars shall fall from heaven, and the powers of the heavens shall be shaken."*

The sun being darkened, the moon being turned to blood, and the stars falling from heaven are all things that happen when the great day of God's wrath comes (Revelation 6:12-17).

Notice Revelation 12:13-14:

> *"And when the dragon saw that he was cast unto the earth, he persecuted the woman which brought forth the man child. And to the woman were given two wings of a great eagle that she might fly into the wilderness into her place where she is nourished for **a time, and times, and half a time** from the face of the serpent.*

There is that terminology again: "Time, and times, and half a time"—three and one-half years. When Satan is cast down into the earth, he will know that he has but a short time left. He will launch the Great Tribulation which continues for three and one-half years.

Notice that this all occurs simultaneously with the Abomination of Desolation. Until this time the world dictator, the Antichrist, has been ruling by peace and diplomacy. However, when the Abomination of Desolation occurs, the Antichrist undergoes a nature change and begins to rule with an iron fist. Could it be, when Satan is cast out of heaven and confined to the earth, that Lucifer himself will personally possess the Antichrist and will begin to rule the world through him? Whatever the case, these two simultaneous events, the war in heaven and the Abomination of Desolation, launch the Great Tribulation.

# 4

# On the Wings of Eagles

"And to the woman were given two wings of a great eagle that she might fly into the wilderness into her place where she is nourished for a time, and times, and half a time from the face of the serpent"

Revelation 12:14

### Who is the Eagle?

When God refers to the persecution of the woman, Israel, He says that there will be given to her two wings of a great eagle that she might fly into a place where she is protected for three and one-half years from the wrath of Satan. God will provide a place of refuge during the Great Tribulation for those in Israel who will believe the prophecies and act on them. The question is: what do the two wings of a great eagle represent?

The eagle is used as a prophetic symbol in another place in the Bible. Daniel 7:1-7 records:

*In the first year of Belshazzar king of Babylon, Daniel had a dream and visions of his head upon his bed: then he wrote the dream, and told the sum of the matters. Daniel spake and said, I saw in my vision by night, and, behold, the four winds of the heaven strove upon the great sea. And four great beasts came up from the sea, diverse one from another. The first was like a* **lion**, *and had* **eagle's wings**: *I beheld till the wings thereof were plucked, and it was lifted up from the earth, and made stand upon the feet as a man, and a man's heart was given to it. And behold another beast, a second, like to a* **bear**, *and it raised up itself on one side, and it had three ribs in the mouth of it between the teeth of it: and they said thus unto it, Arise, devour much flesh. After this I beheld, and lo another, like a* **leop-ard**, *which had upon the back of it four wings of a fowl; the beast had also four heads; and dominion was given to it. After this I saw in the night visions, and behold a fourth beast, dreadful and terrible, and strong exceedingly; and it had great iron teeth: it devoured and brake in pieces, and stamped the residue with the feet of it: and it was diverse from all the beasts that were before*

21

*it; and it had **ten horns***.

## A beast symbolizes a nation or kingdom

A beast in Bible prophecy is always a symbol of a nation or kingdom. Daniel 7:23 says, "The fourth **beast** shall be the fourth **kingdom** upon earth".

## When will these nations exist?

The nations symbolized by these beasts in Daniel 7 will all exist at the time of the second coming of Jesus Christ to establish his 1000-year kingdom. We know this because, in Daniel 7:9, Daniel saw the casting down of the thrones of human kingdoms and the establishment of the kingdom of God. In verse twelve it states that the nations symbolized by the lion, the bear, the eagle, and the leopard have their **dominion** taken away, at the time that Jesus Christ destroys the Antichrist and puts down the kingdoms of men, but **their lives** are prolonged for a season and a time. This proves conclusively that the nations of Daniel 7 will all exist on earth at the time of the second coming of Jesus Christ. These nations will be allowed to live on earth during the millennium under the reign of Jesus Christ and his church.

## Who are the nations of chapter seven?

When God chose to prophesy through symbols, he chose symbols that would have meaning at the time of the prophecy's fulfillment.

The first beast (nation) in Daniel 7 is a lion. There is a major nation today whose recognized symbol is the lion. In *Webster's Third New International Dictionary* under "lion", it states that the lion is the symbol of Great Britain. An article entitled "After the British Lion, the Russian Bear" appeared in the *Indianapolis Star* on January 4, 1980. The editors of the *Indianapolis Star* know that the symbol of Great Britain is the lion. Almighty God knew in 600 B.C. that one of the nations that would exist upon the earth near the end of this age and at the beginning of His kingdom would have the symbol of the lion.

The second beast of Daniel 7 was a bear. Most everyone knows that the symbol of Russia is the bear. We have already referred to the article in the *Indianapolis Star*, "After the British Lion, the Russian Bear". On the cover of *Time* Magazine, May 21, 1984, a large bear was shown biting the Olympic rings in two. This was used because Russia was boycotting the Olympic games. The editors of *Time* Magazine know the symbol of Russia is the bear. Russia is often depicted in the news media as the bear.

In the prophecy a voice said to the bear, "Arise, devour much flesh." Fulfillment of this portion of the prophecy concerning the bear obviously pertains to the revolutionary forces around the world which have encouraged Russia to push the communist revolution to the four corners of the globe. Over the last 50 years, Russia certainly has "devoured much flesh". She has invaded and controlled the Baltic nations, all of Eastern Europe, and Afghanistan. Russian leaders have not believed in God, but God knew Russia and spoke of her before she ever came into existence as a nation!

The Bible says that out of the lion were growing eagle's wings. There is a major nation today whose recognized symbol is the eagle. Take a dollar bill from your billfold. You will see on the back of the dollar bill the official emblem of the United States of America—the eagle. The cover of *Time* Magazine on October 27, 1980, shows an eagle and a bear, representing the United States and Russia, looking over the globe. Isn't it incredible that symbols used today on the cover of *Time* and other periodicals are the same ones used in the Bible 2600 years ago?!

The eagle's wings were growing out of the lion. Where did the United States come from? This is an astounding prophecy that the United States would come out of Great Britain! Great Britain is our "mother country"! And to think that this prophecy was written in 600 BC, 2300 years before the birth of the United States of America!

Daniel then said, "I beheld till the wings thereof were plucked." Daniel actually saw the American Declaration of Independence from Great Britain that would occur in 1776 A.D. The Scriptures go on to say that the eagle was "made stand upon the feet as a man, and a man's heart was given to it." This refers to the United States adopting the symbol of Uncle Sam.

Notice that a man's heart was given to the eagle. The United States has, in fact, not had the heart of a beast. The U.S. will destroy a nation that pushes her into war, and then after winning the war, she will go back and build her enemy up again. Because the United States has mercy on these nations, they sometimes end up being as strong or stronger than her. The United States should never change from that attitude because it is the attitude of Jesus Christ himself—Love your enemies; do good to them that misuse you; pray for them that hate you and work against you. As long as the United States will follow that kind of a policy, the blessings of God will rest upon us.

These symbols in the book of Daniel were not picked indiscriminately by God. These scriptures specifically state that, when Jesus Christ comes back to establish His kingdom, the nations symbolized by the Lion, the Eagle, the Bear, the Leopard, and the ten-horn kingdom will be in existence upon the earth.

We are not going to discuss the identity of the leopard or the ten-horn kingdom at this time. For a complete explanation of Daniel 7, refer to chapter one of *A Message for the President* (see the **end-time** order form in the back of this book).

This isn't the end of what the Bible has to say about the United States. When we move from the book of Daniel to the book of Revelation, there is another prophecy that contains the same four beasts as in Daniel 7. In Revelation 13:1-2, John saw a beast rise up out of the sea. This beast had the body of the leopard, the feet of the bear, the mouth of the lion, and the ten horns of the ten-horn kingdom. It also had 7 heads—the total number of heads of all the beasts in Daniel 7. The beast in Revelation 13 was a union of all the beasts (nations) that Daniel saw 700 years earlier.

Revelation 13 reveals that the separate nations which Daniel saw will move together into a last day world government.

We are seeing the fulfillment of this prophecy right now under what is being called the New World Order. Since the Iraq crisis, the United Nations has become a bonafide world government. It has whipped Saddam Hussein into line. Now a resolution has been passed against Libya demanding the surrender of the two intelligence agents for the bombing of the passenger plane over Lockerbie, Scotland, in 1988, that killed 270 people. The U.N. is threatening economic boycott or even military action similar to the Iraq action if Libya does not comply with the resolution. World leaders, meeting in the first U.N. Security Council summit in history on January 30, 1992, urged the United Nations to abandon its tradition of non-interference in the internal affairs of countries. Among the leaders issuing this statement were George Bush and Boris Yeltsin. This signals a tremendous leap forward toward acceptance of the U.N. as an enforceable world government!

It is especially interesting that the mouth of this unified beast was the mouth of the lion which represents Great Britain. This is significant because the determination has already been made that English will be the international language of this New World Order. Right now you cannot be a pilot on an international air flight unless you speak English. You cannot work in an international airport control tower unless you speak English. And all international telephone operators must speak English. God has let us know through

Revelation 13 that the international language of the endtime world government will be English!

Notice that the eagle's wings of Daniel 7 are not present in the beast of Revelation 13. What happens to the United States? Why is it not represented in this one-world beast? There are two possibilities.

The first reason could be that the United States is included under the lion since the eagle's wings were originally attached to the lion. This could be true especially since over the last few years American Presidents have been the foremost proponents of this world government called New World Order.

The second possibility is that the United States will not continue its present course toward absorption into world government. This possibility does exists, seeing that the Bible clearly states Europe will be the dominant force in the endtime world government. The balance of power in our world today is definitely shifting to the European Union, the Common Market in Europe over which Germany is exerting more and more influence. The Scriptures seem to indicate that this last scenario is the one that will occur.

## American-Israeli friendship prophesied

Remember that the woman is Israel, and the eagle is the United States. When the Bible in Revelation 12:14 speaks of the woman being given two wings of a great eagle, it appears that those Jews who want to flee Israel in order to escape the pending persecution will be assisted by a massive

American airlift. It is very possible they could be brought to the United States. Is it coincidental, at this strategic time in prophetic fulfillment, that Israel's only friend, the United States, just happens to have the symbol of the eagle?! That same friend just happens to have the mightiest airlift capabilities on the face of the earth!

In July of 1991, Jack Kemp, the U.S. Housing and Urban Development Secretary at that time and a leading contender for the Republican presidential nomination in 1996, led more than 1,000 Christians in a spectacular gathering in Memphis, Tennessee, to support Israel and raise funds for the continued immigration of Soviet Jews to the Holy Land. The rally was held under the banner **"On the Wings of Eagles"** (*Jerusalem Post*, July 13, 1991). It appears that **the eagle** will continue to stand by Israel to the very end!

What an awesome book the Bible is! To see the amazingly accurate portrayal of modern nations in prophecy come to pass in minute detail, reminds us that God still controls the nations of the world and the affairs of men. This prophecy of modern nations proves infallibly that we are very near the second coming of Jesus Christ. Each of us should make absolutely certain that we are prepared. We also should work as we never have before to help as many people as possible to be ready for this greatest of all events!

It is obvious that America has a special role to fulfill in the plan of God for these last times. If America is to fulfill that great destiny to which she has been called, there must be a genuine spiritual revival sweep this nation! We must bow ourselves in sincere prayer and return to a literal belief in God's Word as the sole guide for our lives and the life of our nation. This will not happen if we wait on someone else to do it. You and I must start now!

# 5

# The "Prince That Shall Come"

## Who is "he" that confirms the covenant?

"And he shall confirm the covenant with many for one week" (Daniel 9:27). There has been much dispute over who the "he" is that confirms the prophesied covenant in Daniel 9:27. The antecedent to which "he" refers is "the prince that shall come" in the preceding verse—Daniel 9:26.

Verse 26 states that the **people** of the "prince that shall come" shall destroy the city, and the sanctuary. This part of the prophecy was fulfilled when the Romans led by General Titus destroyed Jerusalem and the Second Temple in 70 A.D. The Bible explicitly teaches that the Antichrist will rule over a revived Holy Roman Empire (See *A Message for the President*, chapter 5). It is easy to understand why the Romans were called the "people" of the **prince that shall come**. The "prince that shall come" is the Antichrist, and the Antichrist is the "he" that shall confirm the

30

covenant for seven years.

Daniel 11:21-45 provides a wealth of information about the Antichrist. It calls him the "prince of the covenant" in verse 22. It states that he will "have intelligence with them that forsake the holy covenant" in verse 30. And in verse 31 it says that he will take away the daily sacrifice, and place the Abomination of Desolation.

Finally in verse 45, it says that "he shall plant the tabernacles of his palace between the seas in the glorious holy mountain; yet he shall come to his end, and none shall help him."

The "he" that confirms the covenant for seven years is the coming one-world dictator, the Antichrist. We will describe the Antichrist in detail in a later chapter.

# 6

# The Jerusalem Covenant

"And he shall confirm the covenant
with many for one week..."
Daniel 9:27

The Bible prophesies concerning a covenant
that will be confirmed seven years before the
Battle of Armageddon and the second coming of
Jesus Christ to earth to establish his 1000-year
reign of peace. The covenant must pertain to the
status of Jerusalem, the rebuilding of the Jewish
temple, and the resumption of animal sacrifices.
We know this because, when the covenant is bro-
ken, the temple will be desecrated, and the sacrifice and oblation will be made to cease.

A document called the *Jerusalem Covenant*
was drafted by Justice Menahem Elon, Deputy
President of the Israeli Supreme Court. It was pre-
sented to the Jewish people on Jerusalem Day, May
28, 1992, the twenty-fifth anniversary of the reuni-
fication of Jerusalem. Since Jerusalem was reuni-
fied by the 1967 Six-Day War, Jerusalem Day has
been made an official national holiday in Israel.

The *Jerusalem Covenant* was circulated among world Jewry throughout the world for one year. It was returned to Jerusalem for final signing on Jerusalem Day—May 19, 1993. Cabinet ministers, members of Israel's Knesset (Israel's Congress), and officials of the Israeli Defense Forces and police brass, were among the 1,500 attending the signing of the *Jerusalem Covenant*. The ceremony was marked by massive marches and solemn memorial services throughout Jerusalem. The covenant was signed by Israel's Prime Minister, President, Head of the Knesset, President of the Supreme Court, both of Israel's Chief Rabbis, the mayor of Jerusalem, and most other cabinet members and high officials.

The *Jerusalem Covenant* declares that United Jerusalem is the eternal capital of the state of Israel and that it must never be surrendered. It reaffirms that Jehovah chose to place His name in Jerusalem making it the spiritual center of the Jewish people. The covenant now hangs in the Israeli Knesset building (See figure 1 for the complete text).

The nation of Israel is divided on many issues. Some want to negotiate with the PLO. Others do not. Some want to trade land for peace, while others do not. But there is one issue on which the people of Israel almost unanimously agree. Almost one hundred percent of Israelis declare that the status of United Jerusalem is not negotiable.

The Palestinians, on the other hand, vow that there can be no genuine peace in the Middle East as long as Israel insists on retaining absolute sovereignty over all of Jerusalem. United Nations resolutions 242 and 338 call for Israel to withdraw from territories occupied during the 1967 War in exchange for peace within secure borders. Since East Jerusalem is part of these territories, the world's countries, including the United States, have refused to place their embassies in Jerusalem even though it is Israel's declared capital.

Most problems between Israel and the Arabs appear to be solvable. The final hurdle that seems to stand in the way of a permanent peace is the status of Jerusalem. When the peace talks began in Madrid, Spain, on October of 1991, it was agreed that Jerusalem was not to be discussed during the first stage of the talks. The Golan Heights and an interim agreement on Palestinian autonomy were to be the main areas of discussion. If an agreement on autonomy could be reached, then the future borders of Israel and possibly of a Palestinian state would be negotiated in the next stage of talks to begin no later than the beginning of the third year. In the last few months, however, the Palestinians have relentlessly insisted that the final status of Jerusalem must be discussed now. This is probably one of the main factors that provoked leaders in Israel to enter into the *Jerusalem Covenant*.

Isn't it amazing that a covenant concerning Jerusalem would be signed exactly seven years before the year 2000! It appears that the *Jerusalem Covenant* is the covenant of Daniel 9:27 which the Antichrist will confirm!

# THE COVENANT OF JERUSALEM

## THE FOLLOWING GIVES THE ENTIRE TEXT OF THE COVENANT OF JERUSALEM, AFFIRMED BY JEWS ALL OVER THE WORLD.

### AS OF THIS DAY...

Jerusalem Day, the twenty-eighth day of the month of Iyar in the year five thousand seven hundred fifty-two; one thousand nine hundred and twenty-two years after the destruction of the Second Temple; forty-four years since the founding of the State of Israel; twenty-five years since the Six Day War during which the Israel Defense Forces, in defense of our very existence, restored the Temple Mount and the unity of Jerusalem; twelve years since the Knesset of Israel re-established Jerusalem, "unified and whole," as the "Capital of Israel", "the State of Israel is the State of the Jewish People" and the Capital of the People of Israel. We have gathered together in Zion, sovereign national officials and leaders of our communities everywhere to enter into a covenant with Jerusalem, as was done by the leaders of our nation and all the people of Israel upon Israel's return to our Land from the Babylonian exile wherein the people and their leaders vowed to "dwell in Jerusalem, the Holy City."

### ONCE AGAIN...

"Our feet stand within your gates, O Jerusalem—Jerusalem built as a city joined together" which "unites the people of Israel to one another," and "links heavenly Jerusalem with earthly Jerusalem."

### WE HAVE RETURNED...

to the place that the Lord vowed to bestow upon the descendants of Abraham, Father of our Nation; to the City of David, King of Israel; where Solomon, son of David, built a Holy Temple and a Capital City; which with time became the Mother of all Israel; a City and the Mother of all enactments of Justice and Righteousness, and for the wisdom and insights of the ancient world; where a Second Temple was erected in the days of Ezra and Nehemiah.

In this city the prophets of the Lord prophesied; in this City our Sages taught Torah; in this City the Sanhedrin convened in session in its stone chamber. "For here were the seat of justice and the Throne of the House of David," "for out of Zion shall go forth Torah, and the Word of the Lord from Jerusalem."

Figure 1

## TODAY AS OF OLD...

we hold fast to the truth of the words of the Prophets of Israel, that all the inhabitants of this world shall enter within the gates of Jerusalem: "And it shall come to pass in the end of the days, the mountain of the House of the Lord will be well established at the peak of the mountains and will tower above the hills, and all the nations shall stream towards it." Each and every nation will live by its own faith: "For all the people will go forward, each with its own Divine Name: we shall go in the name of the Lord our God ever and ever." And in this spirit, the Knesset of the State of Israel has enacted a law establishing: the places holy to the peoples of all religions shall be protected from any desecration and from any restriction of free access to them.

## JERUSALEM...

peace and tranquility shall reign in the city: "Pray for the peace of Jerusalem; may those that love you be tranquil. May there be peace within your walls, and tranquility within your palaces." Out of Jerusalem a message of peace went forth and shall yet go forth again to all the inhabitants of the earth: "And they shall beat their swords into plowshares, and their spears into pruning-hooks; Nation will not lift up sword against nation or shall they learn war any more." Our sages, of blessed memory, have said: In the future The Holy One, the Blessed can comfort Jerusalem only with peace."

## FROM THIS PLACE...

we once again take our vow: "If I forget thee, O Jerusalem, May my right hand lose its strength; may my tongue stick to my palate if I do not remember you, If I do not raise up Jerusalem at the very height of my rejoicing."

## AND WITH ALL THESE UNDERSTANDINGS...

we enter into this covenant and write: We shall bind you to us forever; we shall bind you to us with faithfulness, with righteousness and justice, with steadfast love and compassion. We love you O Jerusalem with eternal love, with unbounded love, under siege and when liberated from the yoke of oppressors: we have been martyred for you, we have yearned for you, we have clung to you. Our faithfulness to you we shall bequeath to our children after us. For ever more, our home shall be within you.

## IN CERTIFICATION OF THIS COVENANT, WE SIGN...

# 7

# The Confirming of the Covenant

## Was the Arab-Israeli agreement of September 13, 1993, the confirming of the covenant?

"And he shall confirm the covenant with many for one week." The wording of the prophecy in Daniel 9:27 leaves open two possibilities. Either the Antichrist himself will be the one who authors the covenant, or else the covenant will come into being and then later be confirmed by the Antichrist. If the *Jerusalem Covenant* is the covenant of Daniel 9:27, and it seems almost certain that it is, then the Antichrist will at some time confirm its provisions. To confirm means: to agree with, to strengthen, or to give approval.

### Mideast peace accord

On September 13, 1993, over 3,000 dignitaries from all over the world gathered on the White House lawn in Washington, D.C. They had come to witness an event that most of them thought they would never see—the signing of an agreement between Israel and the Palestine Liberation Organization.

Peace talks between the Israelis and the Arabs had begun in Madrid, Spain, in October of 1991. Several rounds of talks had been held with virtually no progress.

In June of 1992, Israeli elections were held. The Likud Party led by Yitzhak Shamir had campaigned on the promise that they would not surrender one inch of the territories captured in the 1967 War. "This is the land promised by God to our father Abraham," they said. The Labor Party led by Yitzhak Rabin promised to trade land for peace. They contended that peace could only be achieved through territorial compromise. Dreams of "Greater Israel" based on ancient prophecies of the Bible were only obstacles to peace promoted by religious radicals. The issue was clear cut. When the votes were in, Yitzhak Rabin and his Labor Party had won a smashing victory. Israel had clearly voted to trade land in exchange for peace.

During his campaign Rabin had promised to conclude an agreement on Palestinian autonomy within nine months of his election. After being in office for one year, it appeared that Israel was as far as ever from a peace agreement. The violence from the Palestinian intifada was wearing away at the patience of the Israeli people. An agreement with the Palestinians living within Israel was the most pressing need. The big obstacle blocking this possibility was Israel's refusal to recognize the PLO and its leader Yasser Arafat. Arafat had led terrorists attacks against Israel for thirty years, and Israel wanted no dealings with him. However, it became apparent that he had the loyalty of the Palestinian people. No significant decisions could be made by the Palestinian negotiators towards peace without his approval.

Secretly, Israel made contacts with Arafat through the government of Norway. Secret talks were conducted in Oslo, Norway, and continued between Israel and the PLO for several months. Even the official Palestinian negotiators meeting publicly in Washington, D.C., were ignorant of these developments.

In early September of 1993, the shocking announcement was made that a breakthrough with the PLO was imminent. The next week Israel recognized the PLO as the only legitimate representative of the Palestinian people, and Arafat acknowledged Israel's right to exist while renouncing the PLO charter which called for the annihilation of the nation of Israel. All of this paved the way for one of the greatest spectacles in all of history.

When Yitzhak Rabin, Bill Clinton, and Yasser Arafat appeared on the White House lawn, the whole world looked on in amazement. Speeches were made by Israeli Foreign Minister Shimon Peres, PLO Chief Negotiator Mahmoud Abbas, Norway's Foreign Minister Johan Jorgen Holst, President Clinton, Russia's Foreign Minister Andrei Kozyrev, Yasser Arafat, and Yitzhak Rabin. The historic peace agreement was then signed on the same table used in 1979 by Anwar Sadat and Menachem Begin when signing the Camp David Accords, the peace treaty between Egypt and

Israel. In the midst of the thunderous applause of all the dignitaries present from around the world, Yasser Arafat extended his hand to Prime Minister Rabin. History's most famous handshake sealed the first ever peace accord between Israel and her 3,000 year old enemy the Palestinians (Philistines).

The agreement was only an interim agreement. It called for placing the Gaza Strip and Jericho under Palestinian autonomy (self-rule) by December of 1993. The Palestinians would have control over internal affairs including their own police force. Israel would remain responsible for external security. This interim arrangement was designed to see if Arafat could control the Palestinian militants and if Arabs and Israelis could live peaceably side by side. The agreement also called for negotiations concerning the **final status of Jerusalem** and the West Bank area, to begin not later than the beginning of the third year.

The Arab-Israeli agreement actually confirmed the *Jerusalem Covenant* in that it left Jerusalem in Israeli hands—for the present time. The agreement also committed Israel to do what the *Jerusalem Covenant* said that she should never do—negotiate concerning the future of Jerusalem. Since the peace accord temporarily confirmed the present status of Jerusalem, it can be said to have confirmed the *"Jerusalem Covenant"*. If the Antichrist was present at the September 13, 1993, signing, then we have almost certainly entered the final seven years to Armageddon. If not, he must shortly appear to confirm the covenant at which time the final seven-year period will begin.

41

# 8

# Identifying the Antichrist

"That day shall not come, except there come a falling away first, and that man of sin be revealed, the son of perdition."

II Thessalonians 2:3

In 1993 the world witnessed the signing of the Jerusalem Covenant, the Arab-Israeli peace accord, the establishment of Vatican-Israeli diplomatic relations, the Maastricht Treaty creating in Europe a common currency and a common foreign policy by 1997, and the signing of the global trade agreement, GATT—the General Agreement on Tariffs and Trade. With these historic events fulfilling prophecy at an unprecedented pace, it seems almost certain that the Antichrist will appear on the world scene very soon!

## How will the Antichrist be identified?

The Antichrist is called by several names in the Bible—the beast, the man of sin, the son of perdition, the little horn, and the prince of the covenant, among others. In this modern time, this prophesied world dictator is most commonly referred to as the Antichrist. I was amazed to discover fifty-three specific prophecies concerning the Antichrist in the books of Daniel, Revelation, and II Thessalonians alone. In this chapter we will discuss several of these prophecies in order to develop a profile of this future world dictator who is undoubtedly alive on earth at this present moment!

## The Antichrist is a man.

Some have taught that the Antichrist is a system and not a man. However, Daniel 7:24-25 states that ten kings shall arise. Another king will arise after them and will subdue three of the first ten. This king that replaces three will then wear out the saints of the most High until a time and times and the dividing of time (three and one-half years). Daniel 7:21-22 says that the Antichrist will make war with the saints...until the Ancient of days comes. This king, this man, will make war against the saints until Jesus returns. We can know for certain that the Antichrist is a man.

## He will confirm a covenant for seven years.

Daniel 9:27 states that the Antichrist will confirm a covenant with many for seven years. It appears that the *Jerusalem Covenant*, which was signed on May 19, 1993, is this prophesied covenant. The *Jerusalem Covenant* declares that

Jerusalem is the eternal capital of the nation of Israel and must never be surrendered.

The Arab-Israeli peace accord that was signed on September 13, 1993, did confirm the present status of Jerusalem—for now. If the Antichrist were present for the Mideast agreement signing, then the covenant has almost certainly been confirmed. However, we cannot at this time say whether or not this is the case.

## The Antichrist will arise among a union of ten kings.

Daniel 7:24 prophesies that the Antichrist will come up among ten kings. These kings could undoubtedly also refer to presidents or prime ministers. These ten national leaders will be joined together in some type of federation such as the European Common Market or the Commonwealth of Independent States. Revelation 17:12-13 tells us that ten kings will give their power and strength unto the beast.

## His kingdom will be the revived Holy Roman Empire.

In Daniel 2:31-44 a prophecy of a great image is given depicting all of the kingdoms that would obtain world domination from the time of Daniel in 600 B.C. to the establishment of the kingdom of Jesus Christ upon the earth. The image has five sections, teaching us that five empires would rule the world from the time of Daniel to the time of Christ's 1000-year kingdom. History confirms that there have, in fact, been five empires to achieve world dominion from 600 B.C. until now. The head of gold represented Babylon (604-539 B.C.), the arms and breasts of silver—Media-Persia (539-331 B.C.), the belly and thighs of brass—the Grecian empire (331-197 B.C.), the legs of iron—the Roman Empire (197 B.C.-284 A.D.), and the feet of iron mingled with clay—the Holy Roman Empire (800 A.D.-?).

Notice especially that there is a total change of metal when you move from one segment of the image to the other—except for the last segment. The legs of iron are followed by the feet of iron mingled with clay. This indicates that an element of the fourth world empire would be carried over into the last empire.

This is exactly what happened. The Roman Empire ceased to exist around 300 A.D. The Holy Roman Empire was born in 800 A.D. when Pope Leo III crowned Charlemagne, King of the Franks, as emperor of the Holy Roman Empire. The Roman element signified by the iron was retained, but the clay was added. The clay represented the addition of the Roman Catholic Church. The iron mingled with clay represented the union of church and state that made the Holy Roman Empire what it was.

The Holy Roman Empire ruled throughout the Middle Ages—sometimes very strong and sometimes in decline. Because of the enduring influence of the church, even when the political structure was temporarily weakened, the empire would inevitably endure and ultimately rise again.

This prophecy in Daniel 2 teaches that the ten

nation union which gives rise to the Antichrist will be a revival of the iron and the clay—the Holy Roman Empire. The ten toes of the image represent the final ten kings that rule with the Antichrist. Daniel 2:44 states: "And in the days of these kings shall the God of heaven set up a kingdom, which shall never be destroyed."

(For additional proof concerning the Antichrist and the Holy Roman Empire, see *A Message for the President*, chapter 7.)

## The Antichrist will uproot three kings.

This prophecy is one of the most helpful in identifying the Antichrist because it is so specific. Daniel 7:8 says that a little horn will uproot three of the ten horns by the roots. In this little horn were eyes like the eyes of man, and a mouth speaking great things.

Daniel 7:24 explains this prophecy: "And the ten horns out of this kingdom are ten kings that shall arise: and another shall rise after them; and he shall be diverse from the first, and he shall subdue three kings."

When we see a man rise among a ten-nation union subduing three kings, it will be almost irrefutable proof that this man is the Antichrist.

## His ten-nation union will merge into a world government which he will dominate.

Daniel 7:1-8 describes a vision given to Daniel by God depicting four great beasts—a lion, a bear, a leopard, and a ten-horned beast unlike any creature Daniel had ever seen. Later in the chapter it is stated that these beasts symbolize nations, and that these nations will all exist simultaneously with the Antichrist. The lion represents Great Britain, the bear—Russia, the leopard—Germany, and the ten-horned beast—the future powerbase of the Antichrist.

In Revelation 13:1-2, the Apostle John saw one beast instead of four. His one beast was a union of the four beasts of Daniel 7. His beast had the body of the leopard, the feet of the bear, the mouth of the lion, and the ten horns of the ten-horned kingdom. The prophecy of Revelation 13 plainly teaches that the four separate nations of Daniel 7 will merge into one great world government.

Revelation 13:3 says that all the world wondered after the beast. We are witnessing the fulfillment of this incredible prophecy by the development of the New World Order and the empowerment of the United Nations. It is very likely that the Antichrist will ultimately head the United Nations. (For a full explanation of Daniel 7 and Revelation 13, see *A Message for the President*, chapters one and two.)

## The Antichrist will use peace as a weapon.

A recent issue of *Time* Magazine featured THE PEACEMAKERS, the four world leaders that *Time* chose for its 1993 "Men of the Year". Peace is certainly the weapon of choice for any politician of this era who is ambitious for power. Daniel 8:25 says the Antichrist—"by peace shall destroy many."

# He will be promoted by a miracle-working religious partner.

The Holy Roman Empire has always been led by a political leader and a religious leader. The revival of the Holy Roman Empire under the Antichrist will be no exception. Revelation 13:11-12 describes a personage that looks like a lamb but speaks like a dragon. He will influence the people of the earth to give allegiance to the Antichrist who will be leading the New World Order. Verse 13-14 says: "He doeth great wonders, so that he maketh fire come down from heaven on the earth in the sight of men, And deceiveth them that dwell on the earth by the means of those miracles which he had power to do in the sight of the beast." Matthew 24:24 says these signs and wonders would be so great that, if it were possible, they would cause the very elect to be deceived.

# He will apparently have power, and then lose power, and yet regain it.

Revelation 17:8 reads: "The beast that thou sawest was, and is not; and shall ascend out of the bottomless pit, and go into perdition: and they that dwell on the earth shall wonder, whose names were not written in the book of life from the foundation of the world, when they behold the beast that was, and is not, and yet is."

# The Antichrist will be preceded by seven kings. He will be the eighth.

Exactly how this prophecy will be fulfilled is a matter of conjecture at this time. I'm sure it will become clearer as events unfold. Revelation 17:10-11 says it this way: "And there are seven kings: five are fallen, and one is, and the other is not yet come; and when he cometh, he must continue a short space. And the beast that was, and is not, even he is the eighth, and is of the seven, and goeth into perdition."

# His look will be more stout than his fellows.

Daniel 8:23 adds to this description of the looks of the Antichrist, describing him as a king of fierce countenance.

# Three and one-half years after the confirming of the covenant, the Antichrist will sit in the rebuilt Jewish Temple claiming to be God.

This is the very important prophetic event known as the Abomination of Desolation. At this event the Antichrist will cause the Jewish animal sacrifices, which will have been resumed, to stop (Daniel 9:27).

The Abomination of Desolation begins the three and one-half years of Great Tribulation—the last half of Daniel's seventieth week. Jesus said: "When ye therefore shall see the abomination of desolation, spoken of by Daniel the prophet, stand in the holy place...then shall be great tribulation, such as was not since the beginning of the world to this time, no, nor ever shall be" (Matthew 24:15, 21). The Abomination of Desolation is mentioned in Daniel 9:27, Daniel 11:31, Daniel 12:11, Matthew 24:15, and II Thessalonians 2:4.

## He will apparently be regarded as brilliant.

Daniel 7:8 says that he will have a mouth speaking great things. Daniel 8:23 describes him as "understanding dark sentences".

## The Antichrist will persecute God's people.

Revelation 13:7 says, "And it was given unto him to make war with the saints, and to overcome them." Daniel 7:21 states: "I beheld, and the same horn made war with the saints, and prevailed against them."

## He will dominate the world, but will face resistance.

Many have thought that the Antichrist will control every nook and cranny of the earth. However, this is not true. Revelation 12:14 teaches that, when the Great Tribulation begins, Israel will be flown to a place where she is protected from the persecution of the Antichrist and nourished for three and one-half years. Daniel 11 tells us that the Antichrist will fight at least four wars, two of them during the three and one-half years of the Great Tribulation. If he is in absolute and undisputed control, why is he fighting wars?

Toward the end of the Tribulation, Daniel 11:44 states, "But tidings out of the east and out of the north shall trouble him: therefore he shall go forth with great fury to destroy, and utterly to make away many." From these scriptures we can see that the Antichrist will dominate the world, but his control will not be all-pervasive and absolute.

## He shall honor the God of forces.

This apparently indicates that the Antichrist will control the armaments of the world. Daniel 11:31 says that arms shall stand on his part.

Since entering the new Age of Aquarius, a favorite salutation of the new-agers has become "The force be with you." It is almost certain that the Antichrist will be a New Age disciple.

## The Antichrist will think to change times and laws.

The message of the Antichrist will be change, change, everything must change. Does this sound familiar? Established norms will be without value.

## He will not regard the desire of women.

It has been taught from this scripture that the Antichrist would be a homosexual; and that is possible. However, what is the traditional "desire of women"? It has always been to have children. One of the central messages of the global planners is the need to control population growth. In China today there is a tax penalty on any family that has more than one child. Perhaps not regarding the desire of women refers to an enforced worldwide program of birth control.

## The number of his name will be 666.

There has been endless speculation concerning the number 666. It is not likely that the number 666 will be literally stamped on the hand or on the forehead.

Revelation 13:18 says: "Here is wisdom. Let him that hath understanding count the number of the beast: for it is the number of a man; and his number is Six hundred threescore and six." In Revelation 15:2 it specifically states that 666 will be the number of his name.

We don't know yet exactly how this prophecy will be fulfilled, but it is obvious that there will be people of understanding on earth during the time of the Antichrist who will count the number of his name, and know for certain who he is!

## The Antichrist will be destroyed by Jesus Christ himself at Armageddon.

According to Revelation 17:14, the Antichrist and his world government will fight against the Lamb, Jesus Christ. Daniel 8:25 says that he will stand up against the Prince of princes. This will occur at the final war ever to be fought on this earth—the Battle of Armageddon.

At this time the Lord will consume him with the spirit of his mouth, and destroy him with the brightness of his coming (II Thessalonians 2:8).

The Antichrist will be cast alive into the lake of fire (Revelation 19:20), and he will be tormented day and night for ever and ever (Revelation 20:10).

We will then crown Jesus Christ as King of kings and Lord of lords, and he shall reign forever. And of the increase of his government and peace there shall be no end! Hallelujah!!

# 9

# Is the Antichrist on Earth Today?

Throughout the years men have speculated concerning who the Antichrist might be. Napoleon, Mussolini, Hitler, Stalin, Kennedy, Kissinger and Ronald(6) Wilson(6) Reagan(6) have all come and gone. As a result, some have held those in disdain who would dare even to discuss the subject.

Yet the fact remains that a world dictator will definitely appear on the world scene when the prophesied time arrives. The Bible says that, when the time comes, he will be "revealed" (II Thessalonians 2:3).

All the prophecies that are to come to pass in the endtime either have been fulfilled or are in the process of being fulfilled right now! Since the Antichrist is to be revealed in the endtime of this age, and since we obviously live in that time, we are going to consider several prominent world leaders to see if perhaps the Antichrist is already among us. We will take into account the fifty different biblical prophecies describing the Antichrist that are listed on pages 58-59.

We will especially consider the following questions:

**1.** Is he a man of peace?

**2.** Could he rise up among ten kings or (national leaders)?

**3.** Is his look more stout than his fellows?

**4.** Is he in a position to confirm a covenant concerning Jerusalem (probably referring to the *Jerusalem Covenant* signed on May 19, 1993)?

**5.** Can it be said that this person "was, and is not, and yet is"?

**6.** Could his powerbase include a revived Holy Roman Empire?

**7.** Does he have a close relationship with a prominent world religious leader?

**8.** Is the number of his name 666?

**9.** Does he think of changing times and laws?

**10.** Is he the eighth ruler, preceded by seven?

# 50 PROPHECIES OF THE ANTICHRIST

1. The Antichrist is a man—Daniel 7:24-25.

2. He will confirm a covenant for seven years—Daniel 9:27.

3. He will arise among ten kings—Daniel 7:8.

4. This ten nation union will be a revived Holy Roman Empire—Daniel 2:44.

5. He will uproot three kings—Daniel 7:8.

6. His ten nation union will merge into a world government which he will dominate—Revelation 13:1-2.

7. He will ascend to power on a platform of peace and will by peace destroy many—Daniel 8:25.

8. He will be promoted by a miracle-working religious partner—Revelation 13:11-12.

9. The beast was, and is not, and yet is—Revelation 17:8.

10. The world government over which the Antichrist rules will be a red (communistic or socialistic) government—Revelation 17:3.

11. The Antichrist will be preceded by seven kings. He will be the eighth, and will be "of" the seven—Revelation 17:14.

12. He will have a mouth speaking great things—Daniel 7:8.

13. His look will be more stout than his fellows—Daniel 7:20.

14. He will be of fierce countenance—Daniel 8:23.

15. He will understand dark sentences—Daniel 8:23.

16. He will cause craft to prosper—Daniel 8:25.

17. He apparently assumes world dominating power three and one-half years after he confirms the covenant. He then will continue his reign for 42 months—Revelation 13:5.

18. The Abomination of Desolation is the event that signals the beginning of this final 42 months—Daniel 9:27.

19. He opposeth God—II Thessalonians 2:4.

20. He shall speak marvelous things against the God of gods—Daniel 11:36.

21. He exalteth himself above all that is called God—II Thessalonians 2:4.

22. He will sit in the temple of God—II Thessalonians 2:4.

23. He claims to be God—II Thessalonians 2:4.

24. He will take away the daily sacrifice at the time of the Abomination of Desolation—Daniel 11:31.

25. He shall plant the tabernacles of his palace between the seas in the glorious holy mountain—Daniel 11:45.

26. It was given to him to make war with the saints, and to overcome them—Revelation 13:7.

27. He will make war with the saints for three and one-half years— Daniel 7:21, 25.

28. This time of the Great Tribulation launched by the Antichrist begins at the Abomination of Desolation—Matthew 24:15, 21.

29. During this time the Antichrist will scatter the power of the holy people— Daniel 12:7.

30. He will rule a terrible and exceedingly strong kingdom—Daniel 7:7.

31. Power was given him over all kindreds, and tongues, and nations— Revelation 13:7.

32. His kingdom will devour the whole earth—Daniel 7:23.

33. Arms shall stand on his part—Daniel 11:31.

34. He shall honour the God of forces—Daniel 11:38.

35. He will think to change times and laws: and they will be given into his hand for three and one-half years—Daniel 7:25.

36. He shall prosper—Daniel 8:24.

37. He shall not regard the God of his fathers—Daniel 11:37.

38. He will not regard the desire of women—Daniel 11:37.

39. The mark of the beast will be the mark of his name—Revelation 14:11.

40. The number of the beast is 666—Revelation 13:18.

41. 666 will be the number of his name—Revelation 15:2.

42. All that dwell upon the earth shall worship him, except those whose names are written in the Lamb's book of life—Revelation 13:8.

43. The Antichrist will have an image—Revelation 15:2.

44. His coming is after the working of Satan—II Thessalonians 2:9.

45. He will fight against Jesus Christ at Armageddon—Revelation 17:14.

46. He will stand against the Prince of princes—Daniel 8:25.

47. The Lord will consume him with the spirit of his mouth—II Thessalonians 2:8.

48. The Lord will destroy him with the brightness of his coming— II Thessalonians 2:8.

49. The Antichrist is cast alive into the lake of fire—Revelation 19:20.

50. He will be tormented day and night for ever and ever—Revelation 20:10.

# Yitshak Rabin

There are two things that most people in Israel believe the Messiah will do when he comes: **1.** Bring peace and security to Israel. **2.** Rebuild the Jewish Temple. There is presently no individual on the face of the earth better situated to accomplish these two goals than Israeli Prime Minister Yitzhak Rabin.

## Prophecies Fulfilled

### By peace, destroys many

Israeli Prime Minister Yitzhak Rabin's picture appeared on the cover of *Time* Magazine on January 3, 1994, along with Yasser Arafat, South African President F. W. De Klerk, and Nelson Mandela. These four men were chosen as *Time* Magazine's "Men of the Year". The caption expressed very succinctly why these men were chosen for this honor. It simply said, "The Peacemakers."

Rabin's entire focus since assuming the leadership of Israel's government in June of 1992 has been making peace with his nation's enemies. The historic peace accord signed in Washington, DC, on September 13, 1993, reverberated throughout the world. The Bible says that the Antichrist will by peace destroy many. Many people in Israel believe this peace agreement entered into by Rabin will ultimately destroy the nation of Israel.

# He shall confirm a covenant.

One of the first acts of the Antichrist will be to confirm a covenant. The Israeli-PLO peace accord concluded by Rabin and Arafat did confirm the *Jerusalem Covenant*, in that it left Jerusalem in Israeli hands—for now.

The *Jerusalem Post*, December 18, 1993, reported that a Rabin plan already exists to return most all territories captured by Israel in the 1967 war to Palestinian control. Rumor has it that the control of the Temple Mount, the thorniest problem of them all, will be worked out by a sharing arrangement. Some have suggested that Israel would control the north half of the Temple Mount (the area where Israel wants to rebuild her temple, but which is presently occupied by the famous Moslem mosque, the Dome of the Rock), and the Arabs would occupy the southern half, (presently occupied by the Al Aqsa Mosque). If such an arrangement were concluded, there are well financed forces poised and ready to immediately launch the temple project.

# Was, is not, and yet is

Rabin was the Prime Minister of Israel in 1976. After a short stint in power, he was forced to resign and was succeeded by Menachem Begin. Rabin regained the position of Prime Minister by winning the June 1992 Israeli elections.

# He shall think to change times and laws.

Many changes have certainly occurred under the government of Yitzhak Rabin. He could be said to have changed times and laws.

## There are seven kings: the beast is the eighth, and is of the seven.

There have been seven rulers of the modern state of Israel before Rabin. He is the eighth, but yet is also of the seven. Those who have ruled Israel are: David Ben-Gurion, Golda Meir, **Yitzhak Rabin**, Menachem Begin, Yitzhak Shamir, Shimon Peres, Yitzhak Shamir, **Yitzhak Rabin**.

# Prophetic Requirements Not Met

### Rises among ten kings

It appears highly unlikely that Rabin could fulfill this prophecy of rising among ten rulers. The only possibility would be for a Middle Eastern common market of ten nations to be formed and then for Rabin to become the dominant leader in this union. This would be a highly unlikely scenario to say the least!

## He must rule a revived Holy Roman Empire.

The Holy Roman Empire has always consisted of an alliance between a political leader and the Roman Catholic Church. The ruler of the Holy Roman Empire has always come from Europe and never from the Middle East. Given the 2,000-year enmity that has existed between Israel and the Roman Catholic Church, it is highly unlikely that such a union could be accomplished.

## His look was more stout than his fellows.

This definitely cannot be said about Rabin.

## A close relationship with a prominent world religious leader

Rabin does not appear to have any special ties with any great religious personages. It must be noted, however, that he just established full diplomatic relations with the Pope and the Vatican.

## The number of his name must be 666.

Yitzhak has seven letters, and Rabin has five. Unless there is some way of computing his name that we don't presently understand, the number of his name is not 666.

## Conclusion

Unless presently unforeseen events would totally change the world scenario, Yitzhak Rabin, in spite of some astounding credentials, cannot be the prophesied Antichrist.

# Shimon Peres

Shimon Peres was the prime minister of Israel from 1984 to 1986. He now holds the position of foreign minister and is the second most powerful figure in Israel's government.

## Prophecies Fulfilled

### By peace, destroys many

Shimon Peres has been regarded by many as Israel's most dangerous peace dove. He headed the Israeli delegation in the secret Israel-PLO negotiations held in Oslo, Norway, which resulted in the historic 1993 Mideast peace accord.

### He shall confirm a covenant.

If anyone can be said to have "confirmed the covenant", it would be Shimon Peres. He signed the Israeli-PLO agreement on behalf of Israel. It should also be noted that Peres would be perfectly positioned to facilitate the rebuilding of the Jewish temple.

### Was, is not, and yet is

Shimon Peres has previously served as prime minister of Israel. If Peres would again become Israel's prime minister, it could definitely be said of him, "He was, is not, and yet is."

## He shall think to change times and laws.

Being the visionary and the revolutionary that he is, Shimon Peres would undoubtedly change times and laws if he were returned to power.

# Prophetic Requirements Not Met

### Rises among ten kings

It is very difficult to imagine any circumstances where Peres could rise to power among a union of ten kings. In his new book, *The New Middle East*, Peres proposes the creation of a Middle East common market. Anything is possible, but this just doesn't seem to fit the overall pattern of endtime events.

## He must rule a revived Holy Roman Empire.

The Roman Catholic Church will be a partner in the endtime revival of the Holy Roman Empire. Even though Israel and the Vatican recently established full diplomatic relations, it seems beyond the realm of possibility that Israel and the Vatican would rule the world together.

## His look was more stout than his fellows.

There is nothing in Shimon Peres' appearance that could be construed to fulfill this prophecy.

## A close relationship with a prominent world religious leader

We know of no special relationship that exists between Peres and a world religious figure.

# The number of his name must be 666.

Shimon has six letters, but Peres has five. Unless there is a way to calculate 666 that we don't understand, Peres cannot be the Antichrist.

# There are seven kings: the beast is the eighth, and is of the seven.

We know of no way that Peres could fulfill this prophecy.

## Conclusion

Even as Peres enjoys all the possibilities of Prime Minister Rabin, he also bears the same liabilities. He is an undeniable force in the Middle East and the New World Order. He is one of the world's foremost visionaries. He just fails to fill too many requirements of the Man of Sin.

# President Bill Clinton

He leads the United States of America, presently the dominant force in the New World Order. He definitely favors one-world government. His determined promotion of NAFTA (North American Free Trade Agreement) and the global trade agreement GATT (General Agreement on Tariffs and Trade) testifies to his globalism credentials.

## Prophecies Fulfilled

### By peace, destroys many

The Israeli-PLO peace accord is one of the greatest peace achievements in 2,000 years. It can be argued that Clinton deserves no credit for this accomplishment, but it did happen "on his watch". Since Clinton is only one year into his presidency, his peacemaking or the lack thereof remains to be seen.

### He shall confirm a covenant.

The whole world saw the famous photo of President Clinton's outstretched arms pulling Yitzhak Rabin and Yasser Arafat together. His hosting of the signing of the historic Mideast agreement certainly qualifies him as a confirmer of the covenant.

### He shall think to change times and laws.

We can definitely say that Clinton is changing

times and laws. The central theme of his presidential campaign was change, change, change. The pace of change under this administration is absolutely breathtaking!

# Prophetic Requirements Not Met

### Was, is not, and yet is

We see nothing now or on the horizon that would enable Bill Clinton to fulfill this prophecy.

### Rises among ten kings

The only way Clinton could rise among ten kings would be for the world to be divided into ten regions (which has been proposed). An insurmountable problem is that the Antichrist rises after the original ten is formed. America would most certainly, along with NAFTA, make up one of the original ten.

### He must rule a revived Holy Roman Empire.

America has never been a part of the Holy Roman Empire. There has been talk, however, suggesting a "greater Europe" comprised of America, the European Union, and the ex-states of the Soviet Union.

### His look was more stout than his fellows.

I don't think anyone would accuse Bill Clinton of having a stout look or a fierce countenance. If anything he comes across as the "good ol' boy" from Arkansas.

## A close relationship with a prominent world religious leader

In the early 1980's, President Ronald Reagan established full diplomatic relations with the Vatican for the first time since 1869. This continuing relationship is the only possible fulfillment of this prophecy where Bill Clinton is concerned.

## The number of his name must be 666.

William Jefferson Clinton just doesn't add up to 666, no matter how we look at it.

## There are seven kings: the beast is the eighth, and is of the seven.

Unless some power configuration would develop that we cannot foresee, it seems impossible for Clinton to satisfy this requirement.

## Conclusion

President Clinton would have no problem fitting into the endtime world government, but he obviously does not fulfill the prophecies required of the Antichrist.

# Yasser Arafat

Yasser Arafat formed the Palestine Liberation Organization in 1964. The openly declared purpose of the PLO was to annihilate Israel and capture the land of Palestine for the Arab people. Arafat has been the undisputed leader (some would say dictator) of the PLO since its founding.

## Prophecies Fulfilled

### By peace, destroys many

Arafat is using peace as a weapon to carve out his long-dreamed-of Palestinian state. Many in Israel feel he is using peace to destroy the nation of Israel.

### He shall confirm a covenant.

Arafat is one of the two personages on the face of the earth today possessing the most influence over the future of Jerusalem and the Temple Mount. Israel found out that without Yasser Arafat there was going to be no peace in the Middle East. Arafat can definitely be said to have confirmed the *Jerusalem Covenant* by agreeing that Jerusalem stay under Israeli control—for now.

### Was, is not, and yet is

Two years ago the news swept around the world that Yasser Arafat was dead. His plane had crashed in the Libyan desert. To the astonishment of some and the chagrin of others, Arafat survived the plane crash even though he was seriously injured. Arafat views this miraculous escape as proof that the hand of Allah is upon his life, and that he has a special mission to fulfill.

## Rises among ten kings

There are ten Palestinian leaders who presently oppose Arafat's peace activities. It is possible that these ten could change and give their support to Arafat.

## His look was more stout than his fellows.

Of all the world leaders under consideration, Yasser Arafat fulfills this prophecy better than any. With his unshaven face, Arab headdress, and holster on his hip, he definitely stands out among other world leaders.

## The number of his name must be 666.

When Yasser Arafat was exalted into world prominence, I could not help but notice: Yasser has six letters, and Arafat has six letters. But what is his middle name? My staff contacted someone at the Arab embassy who claimed that Arafat does not have a middle name. We have since discovered that he was born Rahman Abdul Rauf Arafat-al-Qudwa al-Husseini (See *Peace or Armageddon?* by Dan O'Neill and Don Wagner). He picked up the nickname Yasser as a boy. He now goes by Yasser Arafat.

The first of Arafat's names at birth was Rahman. Rahman Yasser Arafat would certainly equal 666. If this is not the fulfillment of this prophecy, it certainly is intriguing!

## He shall think to change times and laws.

If Arafat came to world power, you can be assured that he would change times and laws!

# Prophetic requirements not met

## He must rule a revived Holy Roman Empire.

It is difficult to imagine at this point how Yasser Arafat could possibly ascend to the head of the revived Holy Roman Empire. It should be noted, however, that the countries of Europe have historically been anti-semitic and pro-Arab.

## A close relationship with a prominent world religious leader

It has largely been because of deference to the Arabs that the Pope has waited so long to recognize the state of Israel. Whether this could evolve into a special partnership between Arafat and the Pope remains to be seen.

## There are seven kings: the beast is the eighth, and is of the seven.

We cannot envision any way that Arafat could fulfill this prophecy.

# Conclusion

It seems impossible that Yasser Arafat could be the Antichrist. Yet, there are some incredible things about this man. He cannot be completely disregarded.

# King Juan Carlos

Juan Carlos is the king of Spain. Since the Middle Ages the kings of Spain have carried the additional title of "King of Jerusalem." For centuries Popes have recognized the "Catholic Kings" of Spain as "protectors of Catholic Holy Land interests." There are those who adamantly contend that Carlos is the Antichrist.

# Prophecies Fulfilled

## By peace, destroys many

The crowning peace achievement of Juan Carlos, to date, is the hosting of the Mideast Peace negotiations. When U.S. Secretary of State James Baker convened these historic talks in October of 1991, the first site used was Madrid, Spain.

## He shall confirm a covenant.

We have no evidence at this time that King Juan Carlos has been involved with the *Jerusalem Covenant*. However, it is more than interesting that King Carlos and his wife spent several days in Israel in November of 1993. Some suspect that he may have added his signature to the *Jerusalem Covenant* at this time. However, there is no proof for this.

## Rises among ten kings

Carlos is one of the twelve leaders of the

European Community. These twelve nations have agreed to have a common currency and a common foreign policy by 1997. The only problem is that the Bible prophesies a confederation of ten nations, not twelve. If the European Community is to become the powerbase of the Antichrist, its membership must somehow be reduced to ten.

## He must rule a revived Holy Roman Empire.

King Juan Carlos was born in Rome on January 5, 1938. He rules one of the twelve member countries of the European Community, the multi-nation union most likely to become the powerbase of the Antichrist. He also is a practicing Roman Catholic from birth. Carlos was made an honorary citizen of Rome during a ceremony in 1981 at the city council chambers. All of these factors would perfectly position him to rule a revived Holy Roman Empire.

## A close relationship with a prominent world religious leader

King Juan Carlos' coronation took place in 1975. At that time the archbishop of Madrid, Cardinal Vincente Enrique y Tarancon celebrated the mass and bestowed the blessings of the church upon Juan Carlos. Carlos has had several private audiences with the Pope. Throughout history Spain has been one of the foremost strongholds of Roman Catholicism.

# Prophetic Requirements Not Met

# Was, is not, and yet is

We do not see, at this time, any way that Juan Carlos could have fulfilled this prophecy.

## His look was more stout than his fellows.

Unless there is a dimension to Juan Carlos that we haven't yet seen, this prophecy would seem to eliminate him from Antichrist contention. It is significant that Juan Carlos has extensive military training.

## The number of his name must be 666.

We can't presently see how the name of Juan Carlos could number 666.

## He shall think to change times and laws.

We know of no evidence that Carlos has been a changer of times and laws.

## There are seven kings: the beast is the eighth, and is of the seven.

There have been many more than eight rulers of Spain. The only way we could speculate that Juan Carlos might fulfill this prophecy is if it refers to the major rulers of the Holy Roman Empire throughout the ages.

## Conclusion

Although some factors make the case very strong for King Juan Carlos to be the Antichrist, yet other factors make the possibility very remote, if not impossible.

# Mikhail Gorbachev

Daniel 7:7 prophesies concerning the ten-horned kingdom of the Antichrist. That kingdom is symbolized by a dreadful and terrible beast that had **great iron teeth**. When Andrei Gromyko nominated Mikhail Gorbachev to become the head of the Politburo of the Soviet Union in 1985, he said, "Comrades, this man has a nice smile, but he's got iron teeth." In October of 1987, *Readers' Digest* immortalized the nickname forever with the article, "Gorbachev: The Man With a Nice Smile and Iron Teeth." What are the odds that a world dominating politician of Gorbachev's stature would appear on the world scene at this strategic time in prophetic fulfillment and then be described as having iron teeth? Have you ever known of any politician in the history of the entire world to be described as having iron teeth?

I stated in my book, *A Message for the President*, which was published in 1986, that the man responsible for tearing down the Berlin Wall would probably be the Antichrist. Gorbachev was awarded the Nobel Peace Prize for tearing down the Berlin Wall.

## Prophecies Fulfilled

### By peace, destroys many

From 1945 to 1989 the world lived under the icy grip of the cold war. Nuclear war was a very real threat that haunted every living human being upon the face of the earth. In 1985 Mikhail Gorbachev came to power. No one would have believed that four short years later the Berlin Wall would come down, the Cold War would be over, and the countries of Eastern Europe would be liberated. Gorbachev was awarded the Nobel Peace Prize in 1989, and then was named *Time* Magazine's "Man of the Decade". No other man on the face of the earth today can be said to have contributed so much to peace on earth as Gorbachev.

## Was, is not, and yet is

*Time* Magazine May 25, 1992, reported on a one hour visit with the Gorbachevs. The article was concluded with this statement: "He may see himself as the once and future President." If Gorbachev came back to power, this prophecy would be fulfilled.

## His look was more stout than his fellows.

Gorbachev is a stout looking man. And who has not felt a small shiver run down the spine when seeing the large birthmark on his forehead?!

## Rises among ten kings

When the Soviet Union first disintegrated, there were ten of the ex-Soviet states that planned to form the Commonwealth of Independent States with Gorbachev. If Gorbachev ever did return to power, is it possible that these ten would again align themselves with him?

## He must rule a revived Holy Roman Empire.

When in power, Gorbachev dreamed of establishing a united Europe from the "Atlantic to the Urals." He referred continually to "Our common European home". A small article entitled "Papal Promoter" appeared in *U.S. News & World Report* on May 18, 1992. It stated that Pope John Paul II favors a united Europe, and that he thinks Mikhail Gorbachev would be the ideal man to lead it. If this came to pass, it would be nothing short of another Holy Roman Empire.

## A close relationship with a prominent world religious leader

An article by Mikhail Gorbachev appeared in the *New York Times* on March 9, 1992. It was titled, "My Partner, The Pope." In the article Gorbachev said: "I have carried on an intensive correspondence with Pope John Paul II since we met at the Vatican in December 1989. And I think ours will be an ongoing dialogue...Personally, I would be glad to take any opportunity to continue working with the Pope, and I am certain that this desire is mutual and will prove lasting."

## There are seven kings: the beast is the eighth, and is of the seven.

There were seven leaders of the Soviet Union. Gorbachev was the last and the eighth, and he was a communist like the other seven. The eight past leaders of the Soviet Union were as follows: Vladimir Lenin (1917-24), Joseph Stalin (1924-53), Georgi Malenkov (1953-55), Nikita Khrushchev

(1955-64), Leonid Brezhnev (1964-82), Yuri Andropov (1982-84), Konstantin Chernenko (1984-85), Mikhail Gorbachev (1985-91).

## He shall think to change times and laws.

According to *Time* Magazine, July 29, 1991, Gorbachev has been known to sprinkle speeches with terminology about his vision for a "new civilization" that obeys "new laws and logic." He has raised more than a few eyebrows by his private meetings with Sri Chinmoy, the New Age Indian guru.

# Prophetic Requirements Not Met

## He shall confirm a covenant.

We do not know whether Gorbachev has been involved in any way with the *Jerusalem Covenant* or any other covenant that might be the covenant of Daniel 9:27. Russia is the co-host of the Arab-Israeli peace talks, along with the United States. We do know that Gorbachev holds a very special place in the hearts of the Israeli people. He allowed several hundred-thousand Soviet Jews to resettle in Israel during his presidency.

Israel's popular Hebrew poet, Chaim Hefer, wrote, "Gorbachev is the hero. A tree higher than any other in the forest." Former foreign minister of Israel Abba Eban commented that this view is held more widely in Israel than anywhere else.

When Gorbachev visited Israel in June of 1992, the major newspaper *Maariv* said he was "the most important person who ever visited the land of Israel." While in Israel, he was awarded Israel's most prestigious peace prize.

If Mikhail Gorbachev is the Antichrist, he should certainly get along handsomely with many of the Jews in Israel, but he will have to be involved somehow in the confirming of "the covenant".

## The number of his name must be 666.

How 666 could be derived from Mikhail Sergeyevich Gorbachev is a mystery to me.

## Conclusion

The Bible teaches that Russia will be the dominant force that leads the United Nations armies against Israel at the Battle of Armageddon. Knowing this, it makes a lot of sense that the Antichrist could come from Russia.

In 1987 Gorbachev wrote the book *Perestroika*, outlining his vision for one-world government and peace on earth.

As you can see, Gorbachev meets nearly every one of the prophecies concerning the Antichrist. However, we cannot at this time be absolutely positive because a few things yet remain to transpire. But time will soon tell!

Of this we can be sure! We are living in the endtimes, and, whoever he is, it is almost certain that the ANTICHRIST IS NOW AMONG US!

# 10

## Solving the "Jerusalem Problem"

"Behold, I will make Jerusalem a cup of trembling unto all the people round about...all that burden themselves with it shall be cut in pieces, though all the people of the earth be gathered together against it."

Zechariah 12:2-3

Since the 1967 Arab-Israeli War, disputes have raged over the Golan Heights, the West Bank, Gaza, and Jericho. But of all the complex issues facing the leaders in the Middle East, none compare in difficulty to the "Jerusalem Question".

Israel says she will never surrender control of Jerusalem. "Jerusalem is our eternal capital given to us by God, and we will never again allow it to be divided," they say. After being banished for 2,000 years from their Holy City and each year at Passover prayerfully saying, "Next year in Jerusalem," it is unthinkable to most Jews that they should consent to relinquish control of the very heartbeat of the Jewish nation. Israelis are divided on many issues. But there is one issue on which they almost unanimously agree—Jerusalem must never be surrendered!

At the same time the Palestinians say there will never be peace in the Middle East unless they have at least a part of Jerusalem for their capital.

Even though Israel formally annexed East Jerusalem in 1980 making United Jerusalem their capital, the world community, including the United States, has not recognized this move and has refused to place their embassies there. United Nations' Resolutions 242 and 338 call for Israel to withdraw from occupied lands in exchange for peace within secure borders. In March of 1994, a U.N. resolution labeled East Jerusalem as occupied territory. The United States abstained from this portion of the resolution, but did not veto it.

The Jerusalem dispute is nothing new. Both Jews and Arabs staked claim to Jerusalem when Palestine was partitioned by the United Nations in 1948. The U.N. dealt with the problem then by declaring Jerusalem to be an international city. Israel reluctantly accepted this arrangement, but the Arabs wouldn't accept the creation of a Jewish nation in the Middle East, at all. They launched a war the next day. When a cease-fire was finally declared, Jerusalem was divided with the most coveted part of Jerusalem, the Temple Mount, in Jordanian hands. This state of affairs continued until 1967 when Israel conquered the entire city and the entire West Bank area.

When the Israeli-PLO Peace Accord was signed

on September 13, 1993, this interim agreement postponed dealing with the troublesome Jerusalem question. It provided for negotiations on the final status of Jerusalem and the West Bank to begin not later than the beginning of the third year from the signing of the agreement. Even though the Israeli government has publicly declared that the status of Jerusalem is not negotiable, the fact is that the Rabin government signed an agreement to negotiate the status Jerusalem.

## What will happen?

The Bible explicitly states that Jerusalem will soon be returned to Gentile control, except for the area of the Temple itself. It will be under the control of the Jews, and they will build their Third Temple there. This prophecy is found in Revelation 11:1-2.

> "And there was given me a reed like unto a rod: and the angel stood, saying, Rise, and measure **the temple** of God, and the altar, and them that worship therein. But **the court** which is without the temple leave out, and measure it not; for **it is given unto the Gentiles**: and the holy city shall they tread under foot **forty and two months**."

This prophecy definitely pertains to the end-times. Notice, first of all, that the Jewish Temple will be completed by the time of this prophecy. If there were no temple, John could not be instructed to measure it.

This scripture tells us that the Gentiles will tread Jerusalem under foot for forty-two months (three and one-half years). This refers to the last 42 months before Armageddon during which time the Antichrist will rule the world (Revelation 13:5). Whether all of Jerusalem or just East Jerusalem will be under Gentile control, we can't say for sure. It is possible that the city will be internationalized, making every person on earth a citizen of the "City of Peace". Jerusalem would then serve as the capital to both Israel and the Palestinians.

In order for the Temple to be completed by the beginning of the Great Tribulation (the mid-point of the final seven years), construction would have to begin at least two years before the Tribulation begins. Rabbi Chaim Richman, Director of Public Affairs for the Temple Institute in Jerusalem, said that the Temple could be built in less than two years. It is the Temple Institute that has the architectural drawings for the Third Temple already prepared. We cannot say for certain, at this time, when the Great Tribulation will begin. But if it were to begin by 1996 or 1997 (so that the final seven years would culminate by 2,000 AD), construction on the Temple would need to start by 1994 or 1995.

## Is it possible?

Israeli Prime Minister Yitzhak Rabin has stated that 1994 would be the year for peace in the Middle East. Syria, Lebanon, Jordan, and the PLO have all returned to the bargaining table.

Syria has said that she will give peace in exchange for the return of the Golan Heights which Israel captured in the 1967 War. For a full and genuine peace, Rabin will agree to full withdrawal. Since Lebanon is under Syrian control, when Syria makes peace Lebanon will follow.

Agreement between Jordan's King Hussein and Israel has already been reached. Hussein has merely refused to sign an official agreement until Syria comes to terms.

This leaves the Palestinians. Many obstacles were overcome by the Israel-PLO Accord signed on September 13, 1993. The greatest remaining obstacle is the control of Jerusalem. The population of East Jerusalem is still predominantly Arab. The two Arab mosques which dominate the Temple Mount area present a powerful argument for a continuing Arab presence. Yet, everyone knows that the Jewish nation will not long be content to possess control of its ancient temple site without rebuilding Israel's temple there.

One Jewish scholar believes the original Jewish Temple was not located on the present site of the Dome of the Rock. He believes the Temple was north of the Dome. This presents the possibility of building the Jewish Temple beside the Dome of the Rock without disturbing it. This would certainly produce a cozy ecumenical situation—Jews and Arabs all worshipping together on the Temple Mount. The New World Order has arrived for sure!

There are powerful Jewish forces that adamantly believe the Third Temple must be built on the present location of the Dome of the Rock. In

December of 1993, the *Jerusalem Post* reported that secret talks had been held between Rabin and Arafat concerning the final resolution of the Jerusalem problem. Another publication stated that they had secretly determined the final status of the Temple Mount. Supposedly, Israel will control the northern half, presently occupied by the Dome of the Rock, and the Palestinians would possess the southern half where the Al Aqsa Mosque sits. This would enable Israel to rebuild her temple on its original site.

If this report proves to be true, then the prophecy of Revelation 11:1-2 will be fulfilled to the letter! Israel will control the temple area itself, but the outer court will be under Gentile control. Whether the prophecy is fulfilled by this scenario or in some other way, it will come to pass!

# 11

# The Third Temple

The Third Temple must be built in Israel before the pivotal event called the Abomination of Desolation can occur. Remember that the Abomination of Desolation is when the Antichrist, "Sitteth in the Temple of God, showing himself that he is God" (II Thessalonians 2:3-4).

The Jewish people have been banished from the Temple Mount since 70 A.D. Over thirty years after the crucifixion of Jesus Christ, Titus, the Roman general, invaded the land of Israel and the city of Jerusalem. He destroyed the city, burning it to the ground. The prophecy of Jesus found in Matthew 24 that not one stone would be left upon another was fulfilled by the Roman legions at that time.

From 70 A.D. until 1948, the Jewish people had no homeland. In 1948 the nation of Israel was reborn. However, the Temple Mount was still held by the nation of Jordan. When the temple area was recaptured in 1967, the Jews wept. I talked with Gershon Salomon, one of the soldiers that was on the Temple Mount at that time. He said, when the fighting stopped, the soldiers wept like babies. There was such an awesome presence of God as they stood on the location of the First and Second Temple for the first time in 2,000 years!

The joy of the Jewish people was quickly dashed to pieces. A few hours after the recapture, Moshe Dayan, the Defense Minister of Israel, announced that the Temple Mount would remain under Arab control. The rejoicing of the Jews was turned to sorrow. This action to religious Jews was absolutely beyond comprehension. Some Jews believe Messiah was on the verge of appearing at that time, but this blasphemous action caused him to turn away. Jews still cannot go to the Temple Mount area to pray, to offer sacrifices, and, above all, to build their Third Temple.

The First Temple was built by Solomon the son of King David. That temple was ultimately destroyed in 586 B.C. by Nebuchadnezzar, King of Babylon. The Second Temple was completed by Zerubbabel in 516 B.C. Later it was refurbished and made larger by Herod the Great. This is the temple that stood on the Temple Mount during the lifetime of Jesus Christ. The Second Temple was destroyed by the Roman General Titus in 70 A.D. From then until now, no Jewish temple has occupied the coveted Temple Mount.

## Plans to rebuild

The Jews presently are making plans to build the Third Temple. I personally interviewed Mr. Gershon Salomon, the head of the Temple Mount Faithful. He believes God has called him to rebuild the Jewish Temple and that it must be done before the year 2000. In 1990, Salomon and his Temple Mount Faithful attempted to place the cornerstone for the Third Temple on the Temple Mount. When the Arabs realized what was happening, they rioted. In the resulting melee, seventeen Arabs died. In order to keep the need to rebuild the Temple before the Israeli people, Salomon holds a symbolic cornerstone-laying each year. Because of the 1990 riots, he is not allowed access to the Temple Mount.

Another organization dedicated to rebuilding the temple is the Temple Institute. The Temple Institute is located in Jerusalem adjoining the Western Wall Plaza. They have recreated two-thirds of the vessels and instruments necessary for the reinstitution of Old Testament temple worship. I have seen the priests' robes, the basin for catching the blood of the animals to be sacrificed, and the laver where the priests will be required to wash according to Old Testament instructions. They have the incense that must be burned and the harps for worship. Even as this book goes to press, arrangements are being made to purchase red cattle such as are required in Numbers 19 for the resumption of sacrifice. Ashes from a red heifer of the third year must be mingled with water for the purification of the priests who will minister in the rebuilt temple.

## The ark of the covenant

Rabbi Chaim Richman of the Temple Institute stated that, according to the revered Jewish teacher Mammonides, various treasures from the First Temple are buried beneath the Temple

Mount.

Rabbi Getz, the 82 year old chief rabbi of the Western Wall, said that they know for sure the location of the ark of the covenant, the candlesticks made by Moses, and the stone tablets containing the ten commandments.

Rabbi Shlomo Goren, the former chief rabbi of Israel, said that they were digging towards these items. The Arabs, fearing what would happen if the ark of the covenant and the ten commandments should be recovered, rioted. The Israeli government became fearful and ordered the digging to be stopped.

Matthew 24:15, II Thessalonians 2:4, and Revelation 11:1 all explicitly state that the Jewish Temple will be rebuilt in these endtimes. Can you imagine the effect on the people of the world when construction on the Israeli Temple begins?!

The year 1996 marks the 3,000th anniversary of the founding of Jerusalem. Elaborate plans are under way for a year of celebration of this momentous occasion. Wouldn't the Jews love to dedicate their Third Temple during this 3,000 year anniversary extravaganza!!

When construction on the Third Temple begins, those who understand prophecy and its significance are going to know that we are in the last of the last times. The Jewish Temple will become the most tangible and visible evidence of prophetic fulfillment on earth. Great revival fervor will sweep the church of Jesus Christ, even as the program of the Antichrist gains momentum. Daniel 11:32 prophesied concerning this time: "And such as do wickedly against the covenant shall he corrupt by flatteries: **but the people that do know their God shall be strong, and do exploits.**"

# 12

# United Nations Moves to Jerusalem

"And he shall plant the tabernacles of his palace between the seas in the glorious holy mountain; yet he shall come to his end, and none shall help him."
                                        Daniel 11:45

We know that the Antichrist will move his throne to Jerusalem. We know this because the Bible explicitly states that he will move his throne into the Jewish Temple and set himself up as God (II Thessalonians 2:3-4).

The scenario will most likely go something like this: Once Jerusalem is made an international city, all people of the world will be considered citizens of Jerusalem. It will be the focal point for the unity and the brotherhood of man.

In an interview published in *Parade* Magazine on April 3, 1994, Pope John Paul II said, "We trust that, with the approach of the year 2000, Jerusalem will become the city of peace for the entire world and that all the people will be able to meet there, in particular the believers in the religions that find their birthright in the faith of Abraham."

The time will come when the one-world dictator will have obtained world recognition of his leadership. He will reason in his mind: I am the international leader of the world, therefore, wouldn't it be appropriate for my throne to be placed in the international city of the world— Jerusalem. I am a prophet of peace; I am a man of peace. Why should I not place my throne in Jerusalem, the city of peace? That's the rationale that the Antichrist will use.

There will, however, be a deeper reason behind the move of the Antichrist's throne to Jerusalem. Thousands of years ago God declared that he would place his name in the city of Jerusalem (I Kings 11:36). He planned for it to be the headquarters for the Jewish people on this earth.

Satan always wants to displace God. We have already discussed the future war that Satan will launch in heaven, trying to overthrow God. Since God has placed his name in Jerusalem, Satan will attempt to place his name and headquarters there, and he will succeed for a short time.

It's interesting to note that there have been discussions about moving the United Nations' headquarters from New York City where it is presently located. Having the U.N. headquarters in New York is incredibly expensive. Germany has recently offered free rent to the United Nations if it would move its headquarters to Bonn, Germany. If Jerusalem were to become the world's only international city, wouldn't it be appropriate to consider moving the headquarters for international peacekeeping to this international "City of Peace"?

Several attempts have been made to move armed United Nations' troops into Israel. The Israelis have steadfastly resisted this pressure, knowing that once the camel gets his nose into the tent, soon the whole camel will be in. Israel has repeatedly been censured by the United Nations and understands that she has few friends there. The headquarters of the U.N. observers who are already stationed in Israel is located on a mountain just south of the Mount of Olives. The Jews call this mountain the "Hill of Evil Counsel". How prophetic and how true!

The Antichrist will be a master at capitalizing on public opinion. When the Middle East Treaty is concluded and Jerusalem is internationalized, the pull of the symbolism of that city will be irresistible to him. Shortly his throne will be in Jerusalem preparing for the time when he will move his throne into the Temple, setting himself up as God and declaring himself to be the god of this world.

# 13

# Animal Rights Activist Revolt

When the Jewish Third Temple is built, animal sacrifices will be resumed. Because the Jewish people do not believe that Jesus Christ was the lamb of God which takes away the sins of the world, religiously observant Jews believe they are still under commandment to offer the animal sacrifices of the Old Testament. Because they have had no temple, they have not fulfilled this obligation for nearly 2,000 years. We have previously shown that preparations are being made right now in Israel for the resumption of the Old Testament sacrifices.

When the Temple is completed and the sacrifices resumed, it will seem that a great religious revival is taking place in Israel. To those who know Jesus as the Lamb of God and as Messiah, it will merely be a signpost of prophetic fulfillment.

To other peoples of the world, this offering of live animals will be viewed as extreme barbarism. Environmentalists and animal rights activists will be absolutely incensed as the blood begins to flow from the Temple Mount. Recently a baboon liver was transplanted into a man in order to save his life. The animal rights activist picketed outside the hospital in protest of this cruelty to animals, even though it was being done to save the life of a human being! We are living in a time of escalating influence on the part of environmentalists and animal rights activists.

Can you imagine when the first animal sacrifice is performed? As the Rabbi plunges his knife into the throat of the first animal, CNN carries the story live around the world. As the blood gurgles from the throat of the animal, suddenly the cameras swing to the animal rights activists picketing on the Temple Mount. "Animals have rights too! Say no to 20th century barbarism!" the signs will read. Animal rights activists around the world will march in protest. Newspaper headlines will scream: "Inhumane cruelty to animals!"

The Antichrist will have come to power on the platform of environmental issues. He will not be able to resist the cry of the animal rights activists for long; neither will he want to.

# 14

# The Broken Treaty

"In the midst of the week he shall cause the sacrifice and the oblation to cease."

Daniel 9:27

The roar of the animal rights activists will become deafening! They will be demanding that their one-world political leader, who we know as the Antichrist, stop this bloody massacre of animals.

Another factor concerning the Jews will begin to grate on the nerves of the New World Order leader. It is against Jewish teaching for a Gentile to enter the Jewish Temple. After the completion of the Temple, the Antichrist will have watched while the Jews conducted their elaborate cleansing of the Temple from the presence of Gentiles. The Old Testament instructs the Jewish people to not allow Gentiles inside of their temple. In the New Testament, the Apostle Paul was almost killed because it was rumored that he had taken Greeks into the Temple (Acts 21:28).

The Antichrist will view all of this as extreme Jewish religious exclusiveness. One of his most strongly held views will be that religious conflict has been the number one cause for war throughout history. In order to have peace on earth, he will feel obligated to eradicate all religious exclusiveness. It appears that the Antichrist will be a Gentile. If so, he himself will not be permitted to enter the new temple that will quickly become one of the seven wonders of the world. He will chaff under what he views as this Jewish arrogance.

In the Old Testament Nebuchadnezzar, the king of Babylon, had captured the Jewish people, carrying the "best and the brightest" back to Babylon to be his servants. He also took from the Jewish Temple the beautiful gold and silver vessels devoted to the service of God. He had been warned that those were God's vessels and should be used only in his service. Nebuchadnezzar honored this warning and left the temple vessels in storage.

After Nebuchadnezzar's death, his grandson Belshazzar became the ruler of Babylon. At the zenith of his power, Belshazzar made his famous impious feast. He said within himself, "I am the king of Babylon. I rule the entire world." He decided that this exclusiveness of Jewish control over these golden vessels was ridiculous. He commanded that the sacred golden vessels be brought. As he drank from those vessels, the forefinger of a man's hand wrote in the plaster of the wall: ME'NE, ME'NE, TE'KEL, U-PHAR'SIN.

Belshazzar's knees began to smite together in fear; he knew he had gone too far. He sent for Daniel the prophet who gave to Belshazzar the interpretation of the writing: "God hath numbered thy kingdom, and finished it. Thou art weighed in the balances, and art found wanting. Thy kingdom is divided, and given to the Medes and Persians."

History tells us that the handwriting came to pass that very night. Even while Belshazzar was partying, the Persian armies were invading the city of Babylon. Before the night was over, Belshazzar was dead.

This same disdain for restraint will cause the Antichrist to trigger the Abomination of Desolation. The controlled news media will begin to float the possibility that this wonderful world leader, who is bringing peace to the earth, is the Messiah. When the uproar about the animal sacrifices reaches its peak, the Antichrist will solve the problem by informing the Jews that the need for their sacrifices is over. "I am your Messiah," he will confess. He will then move into the Temple claiming to be God. This infamous event, which both Daniel and Jesus called the Abomination of Desolation, will signal the beginning of the Great Tribulation.

# 15

---

# New World Order
# Turns Ugly

"When ye therefore shall see the abomination of desolation...then shall be great tribulation, such as was not since the beginning of the world to this time, no, nor ever shall be."

Matthew 24:15, 21

Many people believe that the way to peace on earth is to have one-world government, one-world religion, and one-world economy. They say that all wars have been caused by political conflicts, religious differences, and economic conflicts. So if we had one-world government, one-world religion, and one-world economy, we would have removed the basic sources of conflict and could have peace upon the earth. Anyone that opposes this "New Thinking" is considered a threat to the New World Order and consequently a warmonger. This is the convoluted logic that will soon plunge the world into the Great Tribulation. The Great Tribulation will be the time of the greatest religious and political persecution that has ever occurred in the history of the world or shall ever again occur. The thinking of the people of the world is presently being conditioned to accept this "ethnic cleansing" of all those that will not conform to the global thinking of the New World Order.

## Gorbachev wants to stamp out genocide and religious exclusiveness.

Mikhail Gorbachev, in his book *Perestroika,* page 231, listed 19 "Fundamental Principles" necessary for building a New World Order of peace and security. He thought these fundamental principles to be so critical in achieving world peace that he sent a copy of them to every head of state on earth. One of these principles, the extirpation of genocide, is now law in the United States. The curious thing about this is that the Genocide Treaty was bitterly fought and refused passage for forty long years. It was finally ratified by Congress and signed by Ronald Reagan on November 4, 1988. There are two burning questions: why did the Senate resist ratification for so long? and why was the treaty finally ratified?

In order to answer these critical questions, we need to explain what the Genocide Treaty is. It was authored by the United Nations in 1948 and quickly ratified by most of the nations of the world. It was originally formulated as a result of the horrible Jewish holocaust under Adolf Hitler. One definition of genocide according to *Britannica*

*Encyclopedia* is: causing serious bodily harm **or mental harm** to members of a national, ethnical, racial, or religious group. Most all of us would certainly be opposed to persecution of minorities in any fashion. Why then did the U.S. Senate steadfastly refuse to ratify this treaty for forty years?!

Opposers of the Genocide Treaty contended that it would undermine rights of Americans under the constitution and infringe on U.S. sovereignty. Alice Widener in the *Indianapolis Star*, March 1977, wrote an article entitled "Those Entangling Alliances". This is what she had to say about the Genocide Treaty: "President George Washington warned us specifically against entangling alliances. If the United States signs the Genocide Treaty, we Americans would be embroiled in the most entangling alliances imaginable. The U.N. Genocide Convention was drafted in 1948 and has been before our Congress since that time. Until Mr. Carter took office, no president urged the treaty upon us, and for very good reason. Does Mr. Carter know, one wonders, that both U.N. covenants he proposes to sign exclude property rights as human rights? They permit the seizure, confiscation, or nationalization of private and corporate property without any kind of compensation."

Senator Sam Irvin Jr. said about the U.N. Genocide Convention in 1974 that its provisions would "immediately supersede all state laws and practices inconsistent with them, and nullify all provisions of all acts of Congress and prior treaties inconsistent with them." When treaties are signed by our government, they become the highest form of law in the land. That means they take precedence over the laws of Congress and the U.S. Constitution. The scary part is that American citizens accused of the crime of genocide would be tried before the World Court without the constitutional protections that we have so long taken for granted.

This Genocide Treaty was finally signed by our President Ronald Reagan on November 4, 1988, two days before the election of his successor George Bush. It has now become the law of our land. That is what is so alarming! If for 40 years our nation's leaders saw inherent danger to the United States and its sovereignty from the Genocide Treaty, are those dangers no longer present?

In "The Hard Road to World Order", published in the prestigious *Foreign Affairs* Magazine, Richard N. Gardner writes: "We are witnessing an outbreak of shortsighted nationalism that seems oblivious to the economic, political, and moral implication of interdependence." We also see that to form this world government...an end run around national sovereignty, eroding it piece by piece, will accomplish much more than the old fashion frontal assault." The ratification of the Genocide Treaty is part of this planned erosion designed to subject U.S. citizens to a world government, with or without their consent.

## Pope urges adoption of Genocide Treaty

Pope Pius XII, the Roman Catholic Pontiff from 1939 to 1958, in an eloquent appeal for the establishment of a world government, stated, "Catholics...above all...must realize that they are called to overcome every vestige of nationalistic narrowness." (*Vital Speeches of the Day*, December 15, 1959, page 141). In the accompanying commentary it says that Catholics are obligated to insist on the ratification by America of the Genocide pact, and the reorganization of the United Nations in order to make it more consistent with that world institution which Pius XII stated should have "supreme power".

The Council on Foreign Relations issued a position paper in 1959 stressing steps to "build a new international order." Study No.7—Basic Aims of U.S. Foreign Policy states in Article #3, "Maintain and gradually increase the authority of the U.N." Article #4 states, "Make more effective use of the International Court of Justices, jurisdiction of which should be increased by withdrawal of reservations by member nations on matters judged to be domestic."

Both Pope Pius XII and Mikhail Gorbachev listed the Genocide Treaty as one of the necessary components of world government. Is it coincidental that one year after the Genocide Treaty became U.S. law, President Bush declared the birth of the New World Order?!

## Why genocide and "hate crime" laws will enslave the world

Genocide is defined as causing physical harm **or mental harm** to any minority. How would you like to be placed on trial for causing someone mental harm?

Genocide laws are presently being administered in many countries under the name "hate crimes". The term "hate crimes" has rather recently been added to the American vocabulary. Many states now mandate stiffer sentences for crimes that are motivated by hate than for the exact same crime judged not to be motivated by hate. The courts are assigned the unenviable task of determining what the individual was thinking at the time of the crime. George Orwell's "thought police" can't be far away.

Hate laws shortly will go even further. In Canada, the individual convicted of inciting to hate, receives a five year prison term. He doesn't have to shoot anyone, pull a gun, or even touch anyone. All he has to do is speak words that could incite to hatred. Canada has now stated that anyone speaking against homosexuality over the airwaves or in the media can be charged with a hate crime punishable by five years in prison. One Canadian official was asked if reading Romans chapter one from the Bible, where Paul condemned homosexual conduct, would be considered a hate crime. His opinion was that it would be!

These "hate crime" laws are not isolated to Canada. The majority of the earth's nations has been infected by this humanistic, socialistic logic. This type of government has been the norm in the Soviet Union since the advent of Communism. The labor camps and mental hospitals have been filled for years with political and religious dissidents. Just ask Mr. Aleksandr Solzhenitsyn and

Mr. Andrei Sakharov, two of Russia's foremost dissidents under the many years of communistic rule.

The United States has been behind the times when it comes to hate crimes, but we are rapidly catching up. A painting contractor in Oregon was charged with religious harassment by one of his three employees. His crime? Asking the young man to church three times. The employee was awarded a judgment of $3,000. When asked how many times the employer could ask his employees to church without it being religious harassment, the judge answered, "Once" (National Prayer Network, P.O. Box 203, Oregon City, Oregon 97045). So much for freedom of speech, thought, and religion in America! Welcome to the New World Order and its "new thinking" for the global man!

## Religious exclusiveness

Mikhail Gorbachev said that the world must extirpate all religious exclusiveness. This may not sound too bad if you don't understand what Mr. Gorbachev means.

To extirpate means to kill off. Religious exclusiveness is defined as claiming to know the truth and labeling as untrue any beliefs that conflict with that truth. In Israel anyone convicted of attempting to convert a person religiously can be sentenced to five years in prison. Proselytizing, as it is called, is considered religious exclusiveness and a threat to a peaceful society.

People that believe there is such a thing as absolute truth have become labeled as fundamentalists. The term, fundamentalist, is now being used to describe everything, from the Moslem terrorist who car bombs Israelis, to Baruch Goldstein, the Israeli who slaughtered 29 Moslems at the now infamous Hebron Massacre, to David Koresh and the Camp Davidians, to the sincere peace-loving Christian who believes and practices the Bible literally. These all are now being painted as the religious bigots that cause most all the conflict upon the earth. The one-worlders say these religious fundamentalists are the world's number one threat to peace and can no longer be tolerated!

The impetus for stamping out the fundamentalists is provided by continually stating in the media that religion, historically, has been the root cause of most wars. It is true that false religion has caused many wars; however, the true religion of Jesus Christ has never caused one war. Jesus taught his disciples to love their enemies and to do good to them that would despitefully use them. Jesus said, "Whosoever shall smite thee on thy right cheek, turn to him the other also" (Matthew 5:39). Any religion that causes a war is a false religion.

The twisted logic of the Great Tribulation will be that anyone, who will not pledge allegiance to the New World Order and the loosely configured one-world religion based on compromise, will be painted as a warmonger. Pierre Boillon, the Bishop of Verdun, France, when speaking on the need for world government, said: "Therefore we must emphasize the great moral responsibility to empower an international authority to prevent war. The entire world must become aware that, if this institution is to become effective, every nation must **renounce its ultimate sovereignty to this universal authority**. This is an obligation! If nations, if rulers of nations, if public opinion will not accept this renunciation, then they really are voting for war, however beautiful may be their speeches on peace" (See *The Council and the Future* by Mario von Galli, pg. 271).

Yet, to join the global church, will be to renounce the teachings of Jesus Christ. To say that Jews, Moslems, Buddhists, or any other religion must believe in Jesus Christ in order to be saved, is considered religious exclusiveness. But, to not say this is to denounce the words of Jesus himself. He said, If you believe not that I am the Messiah, you shall die in your sins (John 8:24).

You may think that such a system of twisted thinking could never become widely accepted in our world. The truth, however, is that this thinking already permeates our world and is presently the law in many nations. Religious freedom will soon be a thing of the past!

Hitler used anti-semitism to fuel hatred of the Jews. The Antichrist will use the doctrines of genocide, religious exclusiveness, and hate crimes to perpetrate the Great Tribulation upon the world.

# 16

# The Great Tribulation

"And I saw thrones, and they sat upon them, and judgment was given unto them: and I saw the souls of them that were beheaded for the witness of Jesus, and for the word of God, and which had not worshipped the beast, neither his image, neither had received his mark upon their foreheads, or in their hands; and they lived and reigned with Christ a thousand years."

Revelation 20:4

Jesus explicitly stated that it will be the Abomination of Desolation that begins the Great Tribulation (Matthew 24:15, 21). By the time of this event, the Jewish Temple will be rebuilt and the sacrifice and the oblation resumed. The Antichrist will order the sacrifice and the oblation to stop and will move his throne into the Temple, claiming to be God. This action will mark the beginning of the Great Tribulation.

Jesus said this would be a time of "great tribulation, such as was not since the beginning of the world to this time, no nor ever shall be" (Matthew 24:21). To say that the Great Tribulation will be the worst period of religious and political persecution in the history of the entire world is quite a statement when we consider the horrors of Hitler's holocaust, the atrocities of the inquisition, and the persecution of the New Testament church! The Great Tribulation will be Satan's final attempt to stamp out those who remain faithful to Jesus Christ, refusing to bow to the Antichrist's New World Order and one-world religion.

Daniel 7:21 says that the Antichrist "made war with the saints, and prevailed against them; Until the Ancient of days came." Revelation 13:7 describes the Great Tribulation this way: "And it was given unto him to make war with the saints, and to overcome them: and power was given him over all kindreds, and tongues, and nations."

In world empires of the past, undisputed power has inevitably resulted in emperor worship. The same will occur in this final resurrected Holy Roman Empire. Revelation 13:15 says the False Prophet, the religious partner of the Antichrist, will "cause that as many as would not worship the image of the beast should be killed." If people on earth will not pledge allegiance to the world leader, the Antichrist, and join the one-world religion headed by the False Prophet, the wrath of the one-world system will come down upon them.

Jesus said of this time: "Now the brother shall betray the brother to death, and the father the son; and children shall rise up against their parents, and shall cause them to be put to death. And ye shall be hated of all men for my name's sake: but he that shall endure unto the end, the same shall be saved" (Mark 13:12-13).

It appears that the full force of the Great Tribulation begins in the nation of Israel. Jesus said, in Matthew 24, that those in Judea should immediately flee when they see the Abomination of Desolation. He said, "Let him which is on the housetop not come down to take any thing out of his house: Neither let him which is in the field return back to take his clothes." Apparently the Great Tribulation will have been well thought out in advance. Anyone in Israel that is going to escape will have to act immediately.

It is interesting to notice, contrary to prevailing opinion, that the Great Tribulation will never reach some nations. Revelation 12:14 clearly states that, when the Antichrist attempts to make war against the woman, Israel, she will be "given two wings of a great eagle, that she might fly into the wilderness, into her place, where she is nourished for a time, and times, and half a time, from the face of the serpent." If there is a place where Israel is to be protected from the Antichrist, then obviously there will be pockets of resistance on earth where the long arm of the Antichrist will not reach. Daniel 11:41 states that "these shall escape out of his hand, even Edom, and Moab, and the chief of the children of Ammon." The Moab Mountains are in the nation of Jordan, Edom is that ancient rock city in Jordan now known as Petra, and Amman is the capital of Jordan. This prophecy that the nation of Jordan will never fall under the power of the Antichrist is especially interesting when we observe how King Hussein has masterfully straddled the fence in the maze of Middle Eastern politics. It appears he will be successful clear to the end!

Daniel 11:21-45 describes the reign of the Antichrist. In this chapter he fights at least four wars. Two of these are after the Abomination of Desolation during the final three and one-half years of his reign. Even after these four wars, he will have opposition. Daniel 11:44 says, "But tidings out of the east and out of the north shall trouble him: therefore he shall go forth with great fury to destroy, and utterly to make away many."

We can see from the above scriptures that the picture of the Antichrist controlling every nook and cranny of the earth is not an accurate one.

The Great Tribulation will be terrible for the inhabitants of the earth, but it will not last long. Revelation 13:5 tells us that the Antichrist was given power to continue forty-two months. Daniel 7:25 and Revelation 12:14 describes the length of the Tribulation as "a time, and times, and half a time." Revelation 12:6 states that Israel will be protected from the Antichrist for 1,260 days. The three and one-half year reign of the Antichrist will swiftly come to an end at Armageddon. He and his religious partner, the False Prophet, will both be cast alive into the lake of fire at that time (Revelation 19:20).

"He that leadeth into captivity shall go into captivity: he that killeth with the sword must be killed with the sword. Here is the patience and the faith of the saints" (Revelation 13:10).

# 17

# 666

"And he causeth all, both small and great, rich and poor, free and bond, to receive a mark in their right hand, or in their foreheads."

Revelation 13:16

When President Ronald Reagan left office in 1989, he bought a ranch in California. The address was 666 St. Cloud Road. He refused to move into his new home, however, until the address was changed. The address was officially changed to 668 St. Cloud Road, and the Reagans moved in.

The young cashier rang up my purchase at K-mart. The total was $6.66. I heard the young lady say under her breath, "Mark-of-the-Beast." I asked, "What did you say?" Embarrassed, she said, "Oh, nothing." I said, "I was sure I heard you say 'Mark of the Beast'." She grinned sheepishly and replied, "I did."

Most everyone has heard the number 666 and is familiar with the term "Mark of the Beast". Not very many people really know what it is all about.

The Mark of the Beast will be the primary tool of the Antichrist in forcing compliance with the New World Order.

One of the key features of the world government of the Antichrist will be an economic system in which every person will have a number. Without this number an individual will not be able to buy or sell. The problem will be that, in order to obtain this number, one must pledge loyalty to the one-world government and the one-world religion which will by then be established.

The prophecy concerning this numbering system is found in Revelation 13:15-18,

> *"And he had power to give life unto the image of the beast, that the image of the beast should both speak, and cause that as many as would not worship the image of the beast should be killed. And he causeth all, both small and great, rich and poor, free and bond, to receive a mark in their right hand, or in their foreheads: And that no man might buy or sell, save he that had the mark, or the name of the beast, or the number of his name. Here is wisdom. Let him that hath understanding count the number of the beast: for it is the number of a man; and his number is Six hundred threescore and six."*

## The Master Plan

It is obvious that we are moving right now into world government under the auspices of the United Nations. It seems the people of the world have accepted this with barely a whimper.

One of the favorite tools of this United Nations world government is economic sanctions. When resolutions are passed by the U.N. against a nation and that nation refuses to comply to the world government body, the first step to force this nation into obedience is to sanction it economically. Economic sanctions have already been employed by the U.N. many times. Iraq, South Africa, Libya, Yugoslavia, and Haiti are all presently under U.N. sanctions.

Revelation chapter 13 not only refers to economic sanctions on nations, but also prophesies that, in the last day world government, economic sanctions will even be used to control the individual. Such a program as was prophesied 2,000 years ago in the book of Revelation has never been possible until the present time. Not until the invention of the computer was the technology even available. With the rapid spread of point-of-sale terminals, progress toward the prophesied cashless society is right on schedule!

## Forces pushing us toward a cashless society

The writing of checks and the use of credit cards are very expensive. Paper transactions, on the average, cost banks approximately 75 cents per transaction. A check must be microfilmed on both sides by the recipient's bank. It must then be sent to the bank on which it was drawn and again be microfilmed on both sides. Finally, it is mailed back to the writer of the check. A totally electronic transaction, on the other hand, costs on the average of 3 cents per transaction. Some banks conduct as many as one million transactions per day. If all of these were done electronically, an average of 70 cents per transaction could be saved. Seventy cents times 1 million transactions per day would be $700,000 per day that one bank could save. Can you imagine the huge financial savings if you took into account all the banks throughout the country and the world?!

There are other severe problems with paper transactions. One-third of the men in Michigan City Prison in the state of Indiana are there for bad check charges. The problem of check verification and the bouncing of checks is a continual headache to the business community. The big corporations of America want to eliminate what we call "float", the time between receiving a customer's check and being able to draw on its deposit. One large corporation has $10 million in float at all times. If all transactions were done electronically, float would be totally eliminated, and this additional capital would immediately become available to those corporations. Credit cards also have their problems. They can be lost or stolen, and they still require the costly involvement of paper because of the needed signature.

Many proponents of a cashless society have pointed out that we could eliminate almost all thievery by moving our economy to a cashless system. There would simply be no money to steal.

## A cashless society would solve the drug problem.

The biggest force of all driving us toward the cashless society is the horrible drug trade. The drug industry depends on the use of cash to avoid detection by the law. If there were no cash and all transactions had to be done electronically, immediately the trail of the huge amounts of money involved in the illegal drug trade would become traceable. Theoretically, this would drive the drug lords out of business. This argument alone is enough for some people to advocate moving quickly into a cashless society.

Another powerful force in favor of the cashless society is the Internal Revenue Service. The IRS would love for every single transaction to be done electronically. It has already been projected that soon U.S. citizens will not even have to file tax returns. Once all transactions are done electronically, the government will have the ability to know which transactions are deductible and will be able to figure your taxes for you.

Counterfeiting is one more force driving the economic planners of our nation into considering the cashless society. There would simply be no counterfeiting if all transactions were done electronically. In this day of smart cards, when an amount of money can be entered upon a card for use with your personal identification number (PIN), many people say the days of cash are now numbered.

This all sounds pretty good. So what's the problem?! The Bible says that a person who submits to receiving this number can never be saved! Why is receiving this number so wrong? Simply because Revelation 13:15 tells us that the condition of receiving your number will be that you must worship the world government and its one-world dictator. If you do not pledge allegiance to this one-world government, you will not be given your number for buying and selling. You will be placed under personal economic sanction by the New World Order. But to worship this image, and to pledge allegiance to this dictator will be an act of idolatry against God himself.

Revelation 14:9-11 says:

> *"If any man worship the beast and his image, and receive his mark in his forehead, or in his hand, the same shall drink of the wine of the wrath of God, which is poured out without mixture into the cup of his indignation; and he shall be tormented with fire and brimstone in the presence of the holy angels, and in the presence of the Lamb: And the smoke of their torment ascendeth up for ever and ever: and they have no rest day nor night, who worship the beast and his image, and whosoever receiveth the mark of his name."*

# How close are we to the "Mark of the Beast"?

It took from George Washington to 1980—200 years—for the United States government to accrue $1 trillion dollars debt. From 1980 to 1984 we gathered a second trillion. By 1987 our national debt had climbed to three trillion. By 1991 it was four trillion. So it took 200 years to accumulate $1 trillion dollars indebtedness for the U.S. government, but only eleven short years to accumulate $3 trillion more. We are now moving toward a total debt of $5 trillion dollars! Presently it takes all the income tax revenue collected east of the Mississippi River to pay just the interest on the national debt. That line is moving westward at 300 miles per year. By 1998 every income tax dollar in the entire country will be required just to pay the interest on the national debt. There will be no money to run the government. Obviously we will face national bankruptcy long before this occurs.

Why in the world are our political leaders plunging us down the path towards national bankruptcy?! The world planners specialize in creating crises and then benevolently solving the very crises which they themselves created. They are planning one-world economy as the solution to the financial crisis toward which America is being steadily lead. Do you really think it is an accident that we accrued in eleven years three times as much national indebtedness as it took us 200 years to accumulate before that time?! It is no accident! It was done by deliberate design! We are right now being prepared for the new world economy—a cashless society where every person will be controlled by the computerization of the citizens of the world!

One of the problems in moving toward a paperless, cashless society is the need for positive identification of the individual making the transaction. There has to be a signature unless another means of positive identification can be developed. Several ideas have been tried. One of them is fingerprinting of the individual for every transaction. However, this is costly, and the public does not like it. Another possible method that is in use in some areas is voice recognition. Machines can recognize a person's voice print and identify that person from every other person in the world. The technology for this is quite expensive and doesn't seem to hold promise for a worldwide program such as is envisioned.

For some time now, certain scientists have wondered if a number could be permanently placed upon the body at birth. This number would be used throughout a person's life. It would become his personal identification number. This is the answer that seems to offer the most promise.

In the *Successful Farming* Magazine, December 1986, on page B8, there is an article—"Goodbye Texas Cowboy, Hello Computer Cow-spotter." An excerpt from the article states, "The computers at a couple of ranches near San Antonio, Texas, don't ride horses, but they can identify each cow in the combined 1,200-head operation better than even the most experienced ranch hand. All cows at Guadalupe Cattle Company and George McAlister Ranch near New Braunfels and Blanco, Texas, are implanted with micro chips. No larger than a grain of rice, the chips—which are read with a scanner—are inserted under the hide between the hook and pin bones. A few key strokes on a computer and a cow's history appears, including a six-generation pedigree, her calving records, weight ratios, calf performance, physical characteristics, and health history. If she is bred, given shots, branded, or calves, the action is recorded using a computer program called Herd-Soft."

The insertion of a computer chip under the skin is also being used for pets in many places in the country. If your pet is lost, your name, phone number, the pet's name, and its entire medical history are immediately known with the mere wave of a laser beam.

All of these things are particularly bone-chilling when we realize that the Bible prophesies an economic system for the endtimes that will require a number being placed on the body!

Another article illustrating the increasing use of numbers in personal identification was entitled, "Commuters: Put the toll on a tab". "Do you fish for quarters when a tollbooth looms? Drive with your knees? No more. Lasers and low-frequency radio waves are slowly replacing baskets and toll takers. Commuters who have been using the San Diego-Coronado Bridge in California, the Lincoln Tunnel connecting New Jersey and New York and, since July, State Route 470 in Denver are cruising through tollbooths where once they had to grind to a halt. How? With a bar code on the windshield—just like those used on groceries—they drive through restricted booths (traveling as fast as 40 mph), and the amount of the toll is automatically deducted from a personal account."

An article entitled, "Food Stamp Benefits Go Electronic" appeared in the *Palladium-Item* Newspaper, Richmond, Indiana, December 21, 1991. It said, "Card-carrying customers simply slide them through a machine at the cashier checkout and enter an identification number on a keypad. The cash register then tells the machine the size of the bill, and that amount is subtracted from the customer's monthly food subsidy. The store is credited for the purchase. Card holders can only spend what they're allocated. These are the new smart cards being used by the welfare system here in the United States."

In *Good Housekeeping* Magazine, April 1989, an article explaining difficulties with bank cards and personal identification numbers said, "Bank cards and PIN's will soon be a thing of the past, as new cash machines that identify you by your fingerprints or the blood-vein pattern in your hands come into use!"

In the *Wall Street Journal*, August 27, 1992, the following note appeared, "Frequent Fliers, lend a hand, requests the Immigration and Naturalization Service. Next month, it will give out forms at John F. Kennedy and Newark International Airports for foreign and U.S. travelers willing to join a test program for faster processing of arriving passengers. It will use infrared hand scans to help confirm the identity of travelers."

In *Newsweek,* July 31, 1989, we read this about the use of Smart cards for the welfare program, "The U.S. Department of Agriculture will soon launch a pilot program to issue food stamps as smart cards. Each recipient would receive a card programmed with a month's worth of benefit dollars, along with a personal identification number. The shopper would plug the card into a store's computer terminal, which would verify his identity and subtract the purchase from the card's memory chip. The smart cards would stamp out black-market and counterfeit food stamps, as well as eliminate cumbersome paperwork. Smart Cards are already on duty at the Marine Corps Parris Island training base in South Carolina. On payday recruits receive chip based cards rather than cash. When a marine makes a purchase on base, he plugs the card into a small terminal, and the sum is automatically deducted from his pay. The base is, in fact, a cashless economy; even the telephones take smart cards."

The most bone chilling article of all comes from *Readers Digest*, November 1976, "Coming Soon: Electronic Money" by Ronald Schiller. In this article he explains all the benefits of the cashless society. His closing paragraph is the most startling: "In this new totally electronic age, the enforcement of financial obligations will present few difficulties, since failure to pay up could be disastrous. The culprit might even be forced to undergo what Electronic Fund Transfer men call 'plastic surgery'—the cutting off of his bank cards. Economically speaking, **this would make him a non-person.**" If there is no cash, and if an individual's right to trade is suspended by putting a hold on his account in a computer system, this article says that person would economically become a non-person. This sounds startlingly like Revelation chapter 13—without the number a person will not be permitted to buy or sell! If an individual's ability to buy and sell could be suspended for not paying his bills, could it also be suspended for refusing to embrace the New World Order and its conflict resolving one-world religion?!

It is absolutely amazing that a prophecy written 2,000 years ago could foresee the time that such a computerized program would be introduced. Never before in the history of the world has such an electronic cashless society been possible. I want to ask every reader right now, do you have a social security number? Do you know anyone who does not? Is that number required for you to hold a job? Do you have to have that number in order to have a bank account? Do you realize that in the coming cashless electronic funds transfer society, unless you have a bank account number, you will not be able to participate in the economy?

The numbering of our society is now accomplished. This is not only true in the United States of America. This program is being installed throughout the entire world. We can credit these intricate prophetic fulfillments to coincidence if we choose. But Jesus said in Luke 21:28, "And when these things begin to come to pass, then look up, and lift up your heads; for your redemption draweth nigh."

# 18

# Great Religious Revival

"It was the best of times, it was the worst of times, it was the age of wisdom, it was the age of foolishness,...it was the season of Light, it was the season of Darkness."

*A Tale of Two Cities*
by Charles Dickens

After writing the book of Daniel, Daniel prayed to God requesting to understand his own writings. God replied in Daniel 12:9, "Go thy way, Daniel: for the words are closed up and sealed **till the time of the end**."

God informed Daniel that the prophecies he had recorded were reserved for a specific people at a particular time. God chose in his divine sovereignty to place the special tool of fulfilled prophecy in the hands of the endtime church to assist the church with endtime revival. Prophecies that have never been understood before are being revealed now. This is not because we are any more intelligent or more spiritual than those who have previously spent countless hours studying God's word. God simply decided to place this powerful weapon in the hands of the endtime church for the final great harvest! Revelation 19:10 states that "the testimony of Jesus is the spirit of prophecy."

The key to great revival is faith. Faith always produces action. Hebrews 11 tells of the great exploits that have been accomplished through faith. A renewed and heightened faith will be responsible for the prophesied endtime revival just ahead.

Paul used prophecy to convince the Jews to believe. The Bible tells us that he would show them prophetically that, when Messiah would come, he would suffer. After they were convinced, he would then preach to them the sufferings of Jesus and that Jesus was, in fact, the Christ.

Jesus prophesied to his disciples that he would die, be buried, and rise the third day. The scriptures say that he told them this so that, when it came to pass, they might believe.

## The effect of prophetic fulfillment soon to be witnessed

What will happen when construction begins on the Jewish Third Temple? What galvanizing effect will it have on God's people when animal sacrifices begin to be offered again in Jerusalem for the first time in 2,000 years? When the Antichrist is revealed, as II Thessalonians 2:3-4 promises he will be, what crystallizing effect will be produced? If the church understands the prophecies, the effect will be dramatic. According to scripture, the endtime church will be powerful and active.

## Endtime revival is specifically prophesied.

Many don't know what to expect spiritually for these last times. Some are even believing for a great falling away. The Bible explicitly prophesies a great revival for the times just ahead!

In II Thessalonians 2:3, Paul did prophesy of a great falling away. This prophecy has already been fulfilled. Paul further described this falling away in Acts 20:29, "After my departing shall grievous wolves enter in among you, not sparing the flock."

All of this did, in fact, occur. After Paul's death, false doctrine crept into the church. One teaching after another was changed until the church descended into the "Dark Ages". This was the falling away prophesied by Paul. We should not be expecting a falling away now. The Bible does say, "Because iniquity shall abound, the love of many shall wax cold" (Matthew 24:12). But it also says, concerning the time when the Antichrist would be revealed in Daniel 11:32, "And such as do wickedly against the covenant shall he corrupt by flatteries: **but the people that do know their God shall be strong, and do exploits.**" It may be the worst of times, but it shall also be the BEST OF TIMES!!

## Racing the rapture

We are the generation that is destined to race the rapture! The fulfilled prophecies of the endtime will be the greatest generator of faith since the physical presence of Jesus Christ upon the earth! The fervor of the book of Acts will be recreated. In Acts 2:44-47 it says, "And all that believed were together, and had all things common; and sold their possessions and goods, and parted them to all men, as every man had need. And they continuing daily with one accord in the temple, and breaking bread from house to house, did eat their meat with gladness and singleness of heart, Praising God, and having favor with all the people. And the Lord added to the church daily such as should be saved." This same fervor and dedication will soon seize the endtime church!

When the prophecies pertaining to Daniel's 70th week begin to be fulfilled, the people that do understand are going to make absolutely total commitments to the last day evangelization of the world. God's people will sell houses and lands. Millions of dollars will be mobilized for the reaching, one more time, of this generation. Even more important, Christians themselves are going to be totally mobilized for world evangelism. Even as the early Apostolic church worked daily with one accord in the temple and going from house to house, the last day Apostolic church is going to be totally mobilized in one final effort to reach this world for Jesus Christ before the Lord comes.

Daniel 11:33 declares, **"And they that understand among the people shall instruct many."** Our printing presses will run day and night. Every evening, all over America and throughout the world, Bible studies will be conducted as we race the rapture. Even though this will be a time of tremendous evil as the Antichrist closes his trap on this world, yet, in the midst of it all, the Bible emphatically declares that they that **"know their God shall be strong, and do exploits!"**

# 19

# The World's Last War—Armageddon

"Behold, I come as a thief. Blessed is he that watcheth, and keepeth his garments, lest he walk naked, and they see his shame. And he gathered them together into a place called in the Hebrew tongue Armageddon."

Revelation 16:15-16

Armageddon! The word itself sends shivers down your spine. There is something foreboding about it. World War II was supposed to be the war to end all wars. But it wasn't. Armageddon will, in fact, be the final war on the face of the earth. It is at Armageddon that Jesus Christ appears on earth to fight on the side of the outmanned Israeli armies. The world dictator, the Antichrist, will be destroyed by Jesus Christ himself during earth's final battle.

The battle is called Armageddon because it will begin on the Plain of Megiddo in Northern

Israel. The Plain of Megiddo is a natural pass from the Mediterranean Sea through the mountains into the interior of Israel. Because of this, many of the famous battles in Israel's history were fought here. Megiddo was the site of Gideon's great victory over 100,000 Midianites with 300 men. King Saul and his son Jonathan died on this famous battle-field.

Revelation 14:20 prophesies that blood will flow unto the horse bridles, by the space of a thousand six-hundred furlongs (160 miles) during the Battle of Armageddon. If you begin at the plain of Megiddo, move eastward to the Jordan Valley, go down the Jordan Valley to Jerusalem, and then westward into the valley of Kidron just outside of Jerusalem, the distance measures 160 miles.

Revelation 16:12-16 gives a description of Armageddon:

> *"And the sixth angel poured out his vial upon the great river Euphrates; and the water thereof was dried up, that the way of the kings of the east might be prepared. And I saw three unclean spirits like frogs come out of the mouth of the dragon, and out of the mouth of the beast, and out of the mouth of the false prophet. For they are the spirits of devils, working miracles, which go forth unto the kings of the earth and of the whole world, to gather them to the battle of that great day of God Almighty. Behold, I*

*come as a thief. Blessed is he that
watcheth and keepeth his garments,
lest he walk naked, and they see his
shame. And he gathered them
together into a place called in the
Hebrew tongue Armageddon."*

## Euphrates River to be dried up

It is fascinating to note that, according to verse
twelve, the Euphrates River will be dried up in
order for the kings of the east to invade Israel at
the Battle of Armageddon. In the January 13th,
1990 issue of the *Indianapolis Star*, the headlines
read, "Flow of Euphrates to be Stopped".

The Turkish government built a huge dam
called the Ataturk Dam. They stopped the flow of
the Euphrates for thirty days in order to fill up
their new reservoir. At the same time they built a
concrete plug for a diversion channel that they
had constructed.

Never before in the history of the world has the
prophesied drying up of the Euphrates been possible until now. However, as of January 13, 1990,
Turkey can stop the flow of the Euphrates River
with the push of a button. It is also very significant
that Turkey (Togarmah) is one of the countries that
will come down against Israel at Armageddon.

## Nations who will fight at Armageddon

Ezekiel 38 and 39 describe the Battle of
Armageddon and the nations that will fight

against Israel at that time. This army will be a federation of nations. It will be a coalition force fighting under the banner of the United Nations similar to what we witnessed during the Iraq crisis. The United States was the dominant force during the Iraq War, with 23 nations contributing to the coalition forces. At Armageddon, Russia will be the dominant force in the World "Peacekeeping" Force that will come down against Israel. We know this because Ezekiel 38:1-2 specifically refers to Russia:

> *"And the word of the Lord came*
> *unto me saying, Son of man, set thy*
> *face against Gog, the land of Magog,*
> ***the chief prince of Meshech** and*
> *Tubal, and prophesy against him."*

The word "Meshech", according to *Webster's Third International Dictionary*, is the root word for "Moschi". This word "Moschi", is the word from which the word "Moscow" was taken. Of course, Moscow is the capital city of Russia. Tubal is also referred to in this passage. There is a city in Russia which is called "Tobol'sk", and the Tobal River is also found there. All of these names can be traced back to Russia.

Ezekiel 38:6,15 refers to the power that comes from the north. Moscow is due north from the city of Jerusalem. There can be no doubt that this prophecy, about Gog and Magog, Meshech and Tubal, is referring specifically to the people who now inhabit Russia.

The other nations that will join with Russia in

her attack on Israel are Persia (modern day Iran), Ethiopia, Libya, Gomer (Poland), and Togarmah (Turkey). These nations are all specifically mentioned in Ezekiel 38:5-6.

## Does Ezekiel 38 and 39 describe Armageddon?

Some have thought that the prophecy of Ezekiel 38 and 39 refers to a different battle than Armageddon. However, a close examination of this passage will show that it is definitely referring to the Battle of Armageddon.

Ezekiel 39:17 describes the battle this way:

> *"And, thou son of man, thus saith the Lord God; Speak unto every feathered fowl, and to every beast of the field, Assemble yourselves, and come; gather yourselves on every side to my sacrifice that I do sacrifice for you, even a great sacrifice upon the mountains of Israel, that ye may eat flesh, and drink blood.* ***Ye shall eat the flesh of the mighty, and drink the blood of the princes of the earth****, of rams, of lambs, and of goats, of bullocks, all of them fatlings of Bashan. And ye shall eat fat till ye be full, and drink blood till ye be drunken, of my sacrifice which I have sacrificed for you."*

Notice, this is the call of God to the beasts of the field and the fowls of the air to come and to eat the flesh of the mighty and drink the blood of the princes of the earth.

The exact same terminology is used concerning the Battle of Armageddon in Revelation 19:17-18.

> *"And I saw an angel standing in the sun; and he cried with a loud voice, saying to all the fowls that fly in the midst of heaven, Come and gather yourselves together unto the supper of the great God;* ***That ye may eat the flesh of kings, and the flesh of captains, and the flesh of mighty men,*** *and the flesh of horses, and of them that sit on them, and the flesh of all men, both free and bond, both small and great."*

In Ezekiel 38:22, God said: "I will plead against him with **pestilence** and with blood; and I will rain upon him, and upon his bands, and upon the many people that are with him, an overflowing rain, and **great hailstones**, fire, and brimstone."

These weapons that God will use against Russia, according to Ezekiel 38, are the exact same weapons that are contained in the vials of Revelation 16 which are to be poured out at the time of Armageddon. In Revelation 16 there are **pestilences and hailstones weighing about a talent (125 lbs.).**

It is at Armageddon that Jesus Christ will destroy the Antichrist and his world government forces. He will then be crowned King of kings and Lord of lords. Ezekiel 38:23 gives the result of the battle recorded there: "Thus will I magnify myself, and sanctify myself; and I will be known in the eyes of many nations, and they shall know that I am the Lord."

## Why will Armageddon occur?

Why will the nations of the world come against Israel? Most likely, the United Nations will pass a resolution to which Israel will refuse to submit. Russia will say to America, "We stood aside while you whipped our buddy Saddam Hussein into submission to the United Nations. Now you stand by while we force Israel to obey the edicts of the World Community." Russia will be delighted that she finally has maneuvered the United States into a position of forsaking Israel.

While Russia smugly moves to invade Israel, what she doesn't realize is that she is merely a tool in the hands of Almighty God. Ezekiel 38:14-16 says that it is God that will bring Russia and her allies down against Israel:

> *"Therefore, son of man, prophesy
> and say unto Gog, Thus saith the
> Lord God: In that day when my peo-
> ple of Israel dwelleth safely, shalt
> thou not know it? And thou shalt
> come from thy place out of the north
> parts, thou, and many people with
> thee, all of them riding upon horses,
> a great company, and a mighty*

*army: And thou shalt come up against my people of Israel, as a cloud to cover the land; it shall be in the latter days, and **I will bring thee against my land** that the heathen may know me, when I shall be sanctified in thee, O Gog, before their eyes".*

God said that He would be "sanctified" in Gog before all of the nations. Russia will be such a mighty nation coming down against little Israel. The odds against Israel's survival will look absolutely insurmountable. The world will look on, thinking that the end of Israel has finally come. However, God has designed events so that His power will be shown in the eyes of all the people of the earth. The invasion of Israel is not something that Russia is going to plan of her own will. In Ezekiel 38:4, God said that he would put hooks in Russia's jaws and bring her down against the nation of Israel. God will put these thoughts in Russia's mind, so that she will fulfill his will!

Zechariah 14:1-2 describes the events this way:

*"Behold, the day of the Lord cometh, and thy spoil shall be divided in the midst of thee. For **I will gather all nations against Jerusalem** to battle; and the city shall be taken, and the houses rifled, and the women ravished; and half of the city shall go forth into captivity, and the residue of the peo-*

*ple shall not be cut off from the
city."*

As the world government armies move toward
the borders of Israel, the Israeli people will begin
to cry for their Messiah. The scriptures teach that
Messiah will appear, descending from the sky and
planting his feet on the Mount of Olives. The
Jewish people will see him coming and will run to
meet him.

They will fall at his feet to worship him. When
they do, they will notice ugly scars in his feet and
in his hands. According to Zechariah 13:6, they
will say, "What are these wounds in thine hands?"
He will reply, "Those with which I was wounded
in the house of my friends." They will ask incred-
ulously, "You're Jesus?!" He will answer, "I am
Jesus."

Zechariah 12:9-10 prophesies: "And I will pour
upon the house of David, and upon the inhabitants
of Jerusalem, the spirit of grace and of supplica-
tions: and **they shall look upon me whom they
have pierced**, and they shall mourn for him, as
one mourneth for his only son, and shall be in bitterness for him, as one that is in bitterness for his
firstborn." When Israel sees that, even though they
crucified Jesus, he still loves them and has come to
save them, they will fall in the dust in great repen-
tance. They will believe upon Jesus as their
Messiah and savior, and he will graciously forgive
them.

The Apostle Paul wrote of this event in
Romans 11:25-27,

*"For I would not, brethren that ye should be ignorant of this mystery, lest ye should be wise in your own conceits, that blindness in part is happened to Israel, **until the fulness of the Gentiles be come in**. And so all Israel shall be saved: as it is written, There shall come out of Sion the Deliverer, and shall turn away ungodliness from Jacob. For this is my covenant unto them, when I shall take away their sins."*

This dramatic scene on the Mount of Olives will mark the time known as "the fullness of the Gentiles".

## The battle

Zechariah 14:3-4,

*"Then shall the Lord go forth, and fight against those nations, as when he fought in the day of battle. And his feet shall stand in that day upon the mount of Olives, which is before Jerusalem on the east, and the mount of Olives shall cleave in the midst thereof toward the east and toward the west, and there shall be a very great valley; and half of the mountain shall cleave in the midst thereof toward the east and toward the west, and there shall be a very*

*great valley; and half of the mountain shall remove toward the north, and half of it toward the south."*

Because their Messiah has come, Israel will face the approaching armies of the Antichrist without fear. With Jesus will be the raptured immortal church and the armies of heaven. The scene is described in Revelation 19:11-21:

*"And I saw heaven opened, and behold a white horse; and he that sat upon him was called Faithful and True, and in righteousness he doth judge and make war. (12)His eyes were as a flame of fire, and on his head were many crowns; and he had a name written, that no man knew, but he himself. (13)And he was clothed with a vesture dipped in blood: and his name is called The Word of God. (14)And the armies which were in heaven followed him upon white horses, clothed in fine linen, white and clean. (15)And out of his mouth goeth a sharp sword, that with it he should smite the nations: and he shall rule them with a rod of iron: and he treadeth the winepress of the fierceness and wrath of Almighty God. (16)And he hath on his vesture and on his thigh a name written, KING OF KINGS, AND LORD OF LORDS. (17)And I*

*saw an angel standing in the sun;
and he cried with a loud voice, saying to all the fowls that fly in the
midst of heaven, Come and gather
yourselves together unto the supper
of the great God; (18)That ye may
eat the flesh of kings, and the flesh
of captains, and the flesh of mighty
men, and the flesh of horses, and of
them that sit on them, and the flesh
of all men, both free and bond, both
small and great. (19)And I saw the
beast, and the kings of the earth,
and their armies, gathered together
to make war against him that sat on
the horse, and against his army.
(20)And the beast was taken, and
with him the false prophet that
wrought miracles before him, with
which he deceived them that had
received the mark of the beast, and
them that worshipped his image.
These both were cast alive into a
lake of fire burning with brimstone.
(21)And the remnant were slain with
the sword of him that sat upon the
horse, which sword proceeded out of
his mouth: and all the fowls were
filled with their flesh.*"

It will be a horrifying experience to face this
angry KING OF KINGS and his heavenly supernat-
ural army! The prophet Joel described the devasta-
tion that will be wrought by the forces of the Lord:

"A fire devoureth before them; and behind them a flame burneth: the land is as the garden of Eden before them, and behind them a desolate wilderness; yea, and nothing shall escape them" (Joel 2:3). Joel said that this army will climb upon the walls of the cities, climb upon the houses, and enter in at the windows like a thief. He said that, when these soldiers are thrust through with the sword, they will not be wounded. Can you imagine fighting against these immortal armies? As the machine guns of the world government armies blaze away, the soldiers of Jesus Christ keep coming right at you! No wonder blood will flow to the horse bridles!!

Finally, the Antichrist and the False Prophet will be cast into the lake of fire. All opposition to the reign of Jesus Christ will be banished and the kingdoms of this world will become the kingdoms of our Lord and his Christ!!

# 20

# Mount of Olives Coronation

"And his feet shall stand in that day upon the mount of Olives, which is before Jerusalem on the east."

Zechariah 14:4

Scripture teaches that Messiah will descend onto the Mount of Olives when he comes to earth to establish his kingdom. Jews believe that those buried on the Mount of Olives will be the first to rise from the dead and, consequently, the first to see him. People have been buried on the Mount of Olives until there is literally no more room. Such illustrious individuals as Israeli Prime Minister Menachem Begin and publishing mogul Robert Maxwell have made the Mount of Olives their final resting place. It was recently reported that the man who is expected to become the next pope of the Roman Catholic Church, Cardinal Carlo Maria Martini of Milan, Italy, has now purchased a grave site in Israel. As we have previously explained, it is when Jesus returns to the Mount of Olives that Israel will believe on Jesus en masse

148

and will acknowledge him as their Messiah.

At this same time, the authority of all human governments will be suspended, and the divine government of Jesus Christ will take over the rulership of the world. This scene is described in Daniel 7:9,

> "I beheld till **the thrones were cast down**, and the Ancient of days did sit, whose garment was white as snow, and the hair of his head like the pure wool: his throne was like the fiery flame, and his wheels as burning fire."

Concerning this same transfer of power from human to divine government, John said in Revelation 11:15-18,

> "And the seventh angel sounded; and there were great voices in heaven, saying, **The kingdoms of this world are become the kingdoms of our Lord, and of his Christ**; and he shall reign for ever and ever. And the four and twenty elders, which sat before God on their seats, fell upon their faces, and worshipped God, Saying, We give thee thanks, O Lord God Almighty, which art, and wast, and art to come; because thou hast taken to thee thy great power, and hast reigned. And the nations were angry, and thy wrath is come,

> *and the time of the dead, that they*
> *should be judged, and that thou*
> *shouldest give reward unto thy ser-*
> *vants the prophets, and to the*
> *saints, and them that fear thy name,*
> *small and great; and shouldest*
> *destroy them which destroy the*
> *earth."*

Daniel describes this same takeover of power on earth by Jesus Christ and his saints in Daniel 7:21-22,

> *"I beheld, and the same horn*
> *made war with the saints, and pre-*
> *vailed against them; Until the*
> *Ancient of days came, and judgment*
> *was given to the saints of the most*
> *High; and **the time came that the***
> ***saints possessed the kingdom."***

Revelation 5:9-10 also teaches that the church will rule with Jesus on earth during his kingdom:

> *"And they sung a new song, say-*
> *ing, Thou art worthy to take the*
> *book, and to open the seals thereof:*
> *for thou wast slain, and hast*
> *redeemed us to God by thy blood*
> *out of every kindred, and tongue,*
> *and people, and nation; And hast*
> *made us unto our God kings and*
> *priests: and **we shall reign on the***
> ***earth."***

# World dictator destroyed

One of the first things Jesus Christ will do when he comes to the earth will be to destroy the impostor who claimed to be God and Messiah. The Bible tells us that Jesus will destroy the world dictator, the Antichrist, with the spirit of his mouth, and the brightness of his coming (II Thessalonians 2:8).

At the same time the Antichrist's partner, the False Prophet, will be destroyed with him. Revelation 19:20 gives this account: "And the beast was taken, and with him the false prophet that wrought miracles before him, with which he deceived them that had received the mark of the beast, and them that worshipped his image. These both were cast alive into a lake of fire burning with brimstone."

# Satan bound 1,000 years

Scripture teaches that, during the 1000-years of peace under the kingdom of God, Satan will be bound. He will have absolutely no influence on the people of the earth. In Revelation 20:1-3 John recorded this binding of Satan:

*"And I saw an angel come down from heaven, having the key of the bottomless pit and a great chain in his hand. And he laid hold on the dragon, that old serpent, which is the Devil, and Satan, and **bound him a thousand years**, And cast*

151

*him into the bottomless pit, and shut him up, and set a seal upon him, that he should deceive the nations no more, till the thousand years should be fulfilled: and after that he must be loosed a little season."*

Can you imagine a world without the devil?! No wonder there will not be one war on earth for the entire 1,000 years. The husband will love his wife; the father the son; the mother-in-law, the daughter-in-law. Finally—peace on earth, goodwill toward men!

## The church rules the world

The church of Jesus Christ is his bride. When Jesus rules the earth as King of kings, the church will rule with him as his queen. The person that gained five talents in the Biblical parable was to rule over five cities; he who gained ten talents was given authority over ten cities. Jesus said if we are faithful over a few things, he will make us ruler over many things.

All who are in the church will be changed from mortal to immortality at the time of his second coming. During the 1,000-year kingdom of God, the immortal church will rule over the remaining mortals of the world. The entire world will worship Jesus as Lord. Jeremiah 31:34 says that in that day no one will say to his neighbor, "Know the Lord: for they shall all know me, from the least of them unto the greatest of them, saith the Lord: for

I will forgive their iniquity, and I will remember their sin no more."

We don't know exactly what our immortal bodies will be like, but the scriptures tell us we will have a body like unto his glorious body after his resurrection. Jesus could appear behind locked doors, and could choose to be visible or invisible. Distance was no obstacle to him. He could move from one place to the other instantaneously and at will.

## Creation reverts back to its original design

In the original creation, human beings lived to be almost a thousand years of age. Because of sin, life-spans were shortened by God. In the kingdom of God, people will again live almost a thousand years. We know this because Isaiah 65:20 states that a man dying at 100 years of age will be considered but a child.

Originally, all creatures were vegetarians. This will be true again in the restored kingdom of God. Isaiah 11:6-8 says that the wolf will dwell with the lamb, the child will play on the hole of a poisonous snake unharmed, and the bear and the cow shall eat together. The lion shall eat straw like the ox. There will be no more killing on earth, not even in the animal kingdom!

## War, never again!

The elusive goal of world disarmament will be realized during Christ's kingdom of peace. At the blacksmith's shop will be stacks of guns and weapons. Isaiah 2:4 says that men will beat their swords into plowshares, and their spears into pruninghooks: nation shall not lift up sword against nation, neither shall they learn war any more.

Finally, the promise given at the birth of Jesus will be fulfilled: Peace on earth, goodwill toward men. There will not be one war on earth for the entire 1,000-year reign of peace. The promised Messiah, the prince of peace has finally come.

## Jesus is Lord!

What a sight! The King of kings will stand on the Mount of Olives with the repentant Jews at his feet. The Bible tells us that every knee shall bow and every tongue confess that Jesus is Lord! As far as the eye can see, men are bowing before the King of kings. Jew, Moslem, Buddhist, and Christian will all call him Lord.

Around him will be gathered the church of all the ages, resurrected and glorified, singing the song of Moses and the Lamb! The saints of all the ages will sing that great anthem of the church, "All hail the power of Jesus name, Let angels prostrate fall, Bring forth the royal diadem, and Crown him Lord of all." As one by one they march around his throne, they remove the crowns they have been given and place them on his head who alone is worthy. Revelation tells us that on his head were many crowns! What a day! What a celebration! Jesus is finally crowned KING OF KINGS, AND LORD OF LORDS!

# Conclusion

With the tremendous convergence of prophetic fulfillment, there is no doubt that we are now living in the countdown to Armageddon. The *Jerusalem Covenant* now hangs on the wall of the Israeli Knesset. It seems almost certain that this covenant, signed exactly seven years before the year 2000, is the covenant of Daniel 9:27.

It is the "confirmation" of the covenant that triggers the final seven years to Armageddon and the establishment of Christ's 1000-year reign of peace. The signing of the Arab-Israeli Peace Accord on September 13, 1994, may or may not have been the "confirming" of the covenant. We cannot say conclusively at this point. It is intriguing that Daniel 8:14 states that from the vision concerning the daily sacrifice unto the cleansing of the sanctuary will be 2,300 days. From September 13, 1993, when the Peace Accord was signed, to January 1, 2000, is exactly 2,300 days. This may be coincidental, but, if it is, it is an absolutely amazing coincidence!

As we go to press, Israel appears to be merely one or two weeks away from withdrawing from Jericho and the Gaza Strip. According to the Israeli-PLO agreement, this is the first step to total withdrawal from the West Bank. Now that withdrawal procedures and policies are established, future withdrawals should be accomplished quite rapidly.

Prime Minister Rabin has said repeatedly that 1994 would be the year for peace with Syria. The peace talks between Syria, Jordan, Lebanon, and Israel are set to resume in a few days. Rabin has stated for the first time that Israel is ready to dismantle settlements in the occupied territories in order to achieve peace. It appears likely that Israel will achieve a peace agreement with all of her neighbors yet in 1994.

## The Antichrist

The Bible is not explicitly clear concerning exactly when the Antichrist will be revealed. Considering our present stage of prophetic fulfillment, the time can't be far away. Once he surfaces on the world's horizon, the race to the finish will begin in earnest.

## Plan of action

If you have never been born again, you should do so immediately. If you are saved, you should be teaching God's word continually. The scripture urges us to work while it is day: for "the night cometh, when no man can work."

# Introducing... **endtime** magazine

Irvin Baxter, Jr., author of *Mideast Treaty*, is editor-in-chief of **endtime** magazine.

**endtime** specializes where no other magazine does—by explaining today's current events in light of biblical prophecies!

For only $19.95 you can receive 12 exciting fact-filled issues of **endtime** magazine delivered to your home.

# Mideast Treaty

## Greatest Prophetic Fulfillment in 2000 Years

■ Jerusalem will soon return to Gentile control

■ The Jewish Temple will be rebuilt in the near future

■ Is the *Jerusalem Covenant* the prophesied covenant of Daniel 9:27?

■ A massive American airlift will rescue Jews from the Great Tribulation

■ The New World Order will turn ugly

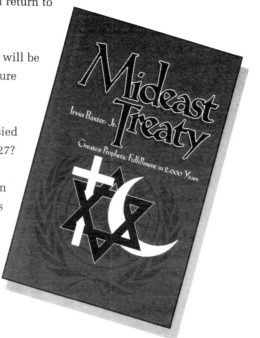

Irvin Baxter, Jr. describes in full detail the final seven years preceding the Battle of Armageddon in this exciting prophetic book.

See the **endtime** order form for more details.

## You will understand the Bible as you never have before!

This is a Christian development course that takes you from Genesis to Revelation in 10 easy-to-understand workbooks.

10 Workbooks $14.50
See Order Form.

Credit Card Orders Call 7 Days a Week 24 Hours a Day
## 1 - 800 - endtime

Other Inquiries Call Weekdays 8:00 am - 4:30 pm (est)
### 1 - 317 - 962 - 8237

Send Mail Orders To

## endtime

**PO Box 2066
Richmond, IN
47375 - 2066**

*Please allow 4 - 6 weeks for delivery.*

# **endtime** Order Form

| BOOKS | Amount | Quantity |
|---|---|---|
| A Message for the President $12.50 * _____ | _____ |
| Mideast Treaty $12.50 * _____ | _____ |

## YOUR BIBLE - A WHOLE NEW WORLD

10 Workbooks $14.50 * _____ _____

## MAGAZINE SUBSCRIPTIONS

Magazine & Gift Subscriptions – $19.95 _____ _____

Canada & Foreign Subscriptions - $24.95 _____ _____

Church Roll (Min. 10) each - $1.00 ** _____ _____

Individual Roll (Min. 10) each - $1.00 ** _____ _____

## TOTALS

\* Canadian & Foreign Add 25% S & H $ _____

\*\* Canadian & Foreign Add 35% S & H $ _____

### Total $ _____

### *Please Pay In U.S. Funds Only*

☐ Enclosed Check or Money Order in U.S. Funds

☐ Visa

☐ MasterCard

☐ Discover Card

☐ American Express

*Charge my Order to this Credit Card Number*

— — — — — — — — — — — — — — —

— — / — —

Expiration Date

Your Name_____

Ch./Co. Name_____

Address_____

City_____ State_____ Zip_____

Telephone # (_____)-_____-_____

*Order Form Can Be Photocopied.*
*Use Additional Paper For Gift Addresses.*

# **endtime** Order Form

| BOOKS | Amount | Quantity |
|---|---|---|
| A Message for the President $12.50 * | _____ | _____ |
| Mideast Treaty $12.50 * | _____ | _____ |

## YOUR BIBLE - A WHOLE NEW WORLD

| | Amount | Quantity |
|---|---|---|
| 10 Workbooks $14.50 * | _____ | _____ |

## MAGAZINE SUBSCRIPTIONS

| | Amount | Quantity |
|---|---|---|
| Magazine & Gift Subscriptions – $19.95 | _____ | _____ |
| Canada & Foreign Subscriptions - $24.95 | _____ | _____ |
| Church Roll (Min. 10) each - $1.00 ** | _____ | _____ |
| Individual Roll (Min. 10) each - $1.00 ** | _____ | _____ |

## TOTALS

\* Canadian & Foreign Add 25% S & H $ _____

\*\* Canadian & Foreign Add 35% S & H $ _____

Total $ _____

*Please Pay In U.S. Funds Only*

☐ Enclosed Check or Money Order in U.S. Funds
☐ Visa
☐ MasterCard
☐ Discover Card
☐ American Express

*Charge my Order to this Credit Card Number*

— — — — — — — — — — — — — — — —

\_\_ \_\_ / \_\_ \_\_
Expiration Date

Your Name_____

Ch./Co. Name_____

Address_____

City_____ State_____ Zip_____

Telephone # (_____)-_____-_____

*Order Form Can Be Photocopied.*
*Use Additional Paper For Gift Addresses.*